MORE
POSTCARDS
from across
THE POND

MORE POSTCARDS

from across

THE POND

Dispatches from an accidental expatriate

MICHAEL HARLING

Second Edition
Published 2012 by Lindenwald Press

© Copyright 2011 Michael Harling

ISBN-13: 978-1461173892
ISBN-10: 1461173892

Author photograph (interior) by Nigel Lord
Author photograph (back cover) by Shonagh Buchanan

For Barbara,
thanks for all the sugar cookies.

Praise for *Postcards*

What a fantastic read! "More Postcards From Across the Pond" is chock full of witty, wry observations that will have any reader—regardless of the place they call home—turning the pages for more. I laughed out loud so many times my husband asked if I was okay.

Marsha Moore, author of the 24 Hours travel series
www.marsha-moore.com

Anyone who's dreamed of or endured life in Britain will love Michael Harling's hilarious and on-the-mark tales in "More Postcards From Across The Pond."

Leslie Banker and William Mullins,
co-authors of "Britannia in Brief"
www.britanniainbrief.com

Mike has that certain "something" about his writing. Entertaining? Certainly. Humorous? Outrageously. Insightful? Definitely. All these and so much more; a gentle wander through the streets of a small southern English town as seen through the eyes of a foreigner who is slowly being assimilated into the British way of life. However, his roots betray him; he "sees" things which totally pass by us ordinary British folk, and then writes about them in a way to charm and delight an audience from either side of the water. I for one am glad to dive into this book headfirst and enjoy every morsel on offer.

Steve Gillen, fan, Yorkshire man, expat spouse

When you have a British sense of humour trapped in an American mind, there are a limited number of career options open to you. Michael Harling has found his niche—taking the piss out of the British in a dry, matter-of-fact and gloriously British way.

Chris Rae, author of "The Septic's Companion"
www.septicscompanion.com

Foreword

I have had the pleasure of co-hosting a blog with Mike Harling for a number of years now, and I never tire of his writing. Master of the understated and unexpected, Mike knows how to tell a story or offer an opinion.

Since he moved to England from the States a lot of things have changed – some good, some bad. Brits now have 24/7 shopping and air-conditioning (after a fashion), and American food is available without too much of a search. Mike ponders all this and more in this welcomed follow-up to his first book, *Postcards From Across the Pond*.

With his trademark mellow, self-deprecating humour, Mike delivers anecdotes and opinions on subjects as diverse as Halloween, home deliveries and tipping in bars. He pokes fun at his own attempts to play cricket, warns Brits about the dangers of Krispy Kremes and tries to get his head around the great British pantomime. *More Postcards From Across the Pond* is an entertaining, thought-provoking collection of Mike's observations on life in the United Kingdom, a place he has clearly come to love.

If, like me, you enjoy reading, with no agenda except enjoyment, I promise you will not come away disappointed.

Toni Summers Hargis, author of *Rules, Britannia!*
www.rulesbritannia.com

Contents

Introduction

After my first book came out (yes, this is the sequel; run out and buy the first book right now if you haven't already, or go out and buy a second copy if you have) I was questioned by a number of readers about just where and, more precisely, when I was supposedly living, arguing that the experiences I related seemed more suited to the post war era than modern day Britain. They stopped short of accusing me of making this stuff up, but you could tell that's what they were thinking.

While I admit to a smattering of exaggeration for comic effect, I am not, I promise, taking the piss out of the British by maintaining the pretence that England is a backward country. Still, when an agent turns down the opportunity to represent your manuscript with the quip, "you'd be hard pressed to find a sink with double taps these days, especially in the south," I think, first of all, that she doesn't get out of London quite often enough, and secondly that, just perhaps, a bit of explanation is in order.

In my musings about encounters with the indigenous population, there are always two conditions that are going to work against them (or three, if you count the fact that I'm always going to focus on the silly stuff).

First, many of my impressions of England were written immediately after my arrival in this quaint market town, during those heady and wonderful days when everything was exotic and new. To read those accounts and come away with the notion that the entire United Kingdom must be as I described it is as logical as believing that a person plunked down in the middle of Nebraska could convey the total experience of modern life in the United States. Britain's terrain, population and customs are every bit as diverse as America's (only smaller) and one person could never speak for them all.

Secondly, and sadly, Britain is changing. (I'm not sad that it's changing, I'm sad because it's changing into America.) There are statements I made in my early observations that, due to progress, are no longer true, and the rate of change is only escalating.

Years ago I wrote of my unrequited yearning for several uniquely American food products that today I can pick up at my local Tesco's. More and more stores are extending their business hours, and now, as in the States, if you suddenly feel the urge for a jar of pickles or a disposable barbeque at three in the morning, you shouldn't have much difficulty locating an open supermarket that sells them.

If you buy a new car, unless you go for the basic economy model, it's likely to come with AC. Putting air conditioning in businesses or homes is still not as popular as in the States but that's only because, traditionally, it wasn't needed. Now that it's hot here more than two or three days a year I am, increasingly, finding myself enveloped in cool, artificial air when I step into a shop. Even my office has air conditioning now. (When you think about it, every building on this island might have had central air conditioning installed long before my arrival, but if it never got hot enough to use it, how would I know?)

Dishwashers are prevalent now and American-sized refrigerators are becoming popular for those lucky few who have the space. Every new or refurbished building comes fitted with double glazed windows and electrical sockets in the bathrooms, and most will have single-tap sinks.

As this becomes the norm, you could be forgiven for listening to me blather on about my flat and come away thinking, "Where does this guy live?" Well, I'll tell you: I live in a 2nd floor walk-up with single glazed windows, double-tap sinks and no plug points in the bathroom.

But that doesn't mean my own, personal Britain isn't changing as well. The quaint and idiosyncratic way of life I championed in those early years is gradually being pushed aside and I can't say I'm 100% sorry to see it go—being cold, uncomfortable and inconvenienced is romantic for about three months but after that instant gratification begins to look more and more appealing.

As you will read in these pages, the vintage storage heaters I had invested many hours coming to terms with when we first moved in finally expired. They were replaced with electric heaters that, when you turn them on heat up, and, conversely, cool down when you turn them off. They were even fitted with timers! We marveled over them for nearly a week until.., well, that's another story.

My wife and I both have mobile phones now and we have a modern, cordless phone in the flat. We also have broadband, a clothes dryer and a 24-hour super-store around the corner.

Sweeping changes abound. My very first train ride in England was in an antiquated "slam-door" rail car. These anachronisms have since been retired in favor of modern carriages and, while the romantic in me is sorry to see them go, I have to admit it's a vast improvement. The juggernaut of modernization has seen many traditional pubs gutted and converted into bar/restaurants, replete with shiny new woodwork, attentive, uniformed staff and the type of decor the owners apparently believe American tourists expect when they visit a "traditional" British pub. Most pubs stay open throughout the afternoons now and, even though eleven o'clock remains the customary closing time, it is no longer the law. Fox hunting is a thing of the past, as is going to the local pub for a pint and a smoke, though that hardly matters now that most of the pubs are gone.

With all this happening within a few short years, it's small wonder my initial impressions of Britain seem dated; but I do not consider them any less valid and certainly not untrue. Perhaps in the distant future (say, ten or twelve years) historians will use them as a guide to what British life was like in "the old days" but, for the time being at least, there are still enough people around for whom smoke-filled pubs and double-tap sinks are within living memory.

So my first book is essential reading, a guide to ancient history for those Britons still looking forward to their first Smart Phone. And I can sympathize with them; my first five years here seem like a long time ago, even to me. This book contains sixty additional adventures set in a more modern version of Britain. They appear, more or less, in chronological order, to allow you to experience the cycle of the seasons along with me and, more importantly, to keep me from having to obsess over which order they might flow better in. I hope you enjoy reading them as much as I did living them.

As for myself, I suppose it's time to let go of the past and start facing up to the fact that I live in the 21st century. I'm rather ambivalent about that idea; I don't find it nearly as funny, but at least I can have a Fluffernutter™ if I feel like it.

Michael Harling
April 2011

Holiday Exchange

The Queen is coming to town tomorrow and the whole place has been in a flurry of activity for the past six weeks.

Thousands of people are going to be bused in to crowd the market square and line the streets in order to maximize festivity, as well provide the appearance of popularity, for the joyous event. All so an old lady can ride through the town, wave to people she doesn't know, mumble a few words of dedication over our new sundial and ride away without remarking on the effort we went through to decorate the place or noticing that practically everything in town is covered with a fresh coat of paint.

It must be odd being Queen; she probably believes that the entire country is decked out in red, white and blue bunting, festooned with flowers, populated by smiling, happy people and smells of fresh paint. But that's not what I want to talk about; I want to talk about the disturbing trend of the British stealing our holidays.

First they started Trick-or-Treating, now they're planning a Harvest Festival Feast. Okay, so it's not Thanksgiving as we know it, but I think it's obvious where the idea came from.

The problem with usurping another culture's holidays is that you only get the outer trappings and tend to miss the underlying traditions, which is why the growing trend of inflicting Halloween on the populace over here is drawing criticism.

Halloween in Britain is wrong on so many levels. First and foremost, they have a perfectly adequate autumn holiday of their own only five days after Halloween called Bonfire Night or Guy Fawkes Day, featuring raucous celebrations, effigy burnings, mischief (or vandalism, depending on your point of view) and fireworks. Granted, they don't hand out free candy, but they could use some of their "Guy" money for that if they really wanted to.

And this leads into the second reason they shouldn't have Halloween here; they have no idea how to celebrate it.

In their current autumnal holiday, it is traditional, during the two or three weeks preceding it, for kids to make a dummy representing Guy Fawkes and sit on street corners with it asking passers-by, "A penny for the Guy?" The idea is to buy fireworks and other burnable materials to set alight on Bonfire Night upon which their dummies, or effigies, of Guy Fawkes, are burned.

This is all well and good; I love traditions and have no qualms about tossing 50 pence into their begging bowls. The locals deal with it as well but tend to grumble a bit more because, "back in my day, we had better dummies, not a Manchester United sweatshirt stuffed with leaves and topped off with a mask!" I guess their fear is that soon this holiday tradition will be reduced to delinquents, holding nothing but an old sock to represent The Guy, and accosting pedestrians for spare change.

This seasonal nature of Guy Fawkes Day—namely the way it starts weeks before the actual event—seems to have been transferred onto their idea of Halloween, making for a decidedly confusing and hybrid version of this autumnal American activity. Children over here, I am told, start repeatedly frisking their neighbors for candy as early as the middle of October, often wearing little more than their street clothes and a mask. That's not Halloween, that's simply a shakedown, which is why so many people here are against the idea, and why the local police hand out signs to stick on your door that say, in effect, "Piss off you little bastards!"

You can't just grab another country's holiday at random and expect to understand the nuances of how to celebrate it and I encourage them to give up on Halloween; if the British want to take one of our holidays, they would be much better off with the 4th of July.

This idea may seem sort of strange, but the Revolutionary War and its outcome are no surprise to the residents over here and it represents, after all, an excuse to get drunk, set off fireworks and, most importantly, provide another summer bank holiday. Over here, you see, our legal holidays fall in an unfortunate pattern. After the Christmas-New Year-Easter run, we've got May Day, on the first of May, Whitsun at the end of May, and then nothing substantial until Christmas. Guy Fawkes Day, like Halloween, isn't a legal holiday and, over here, they don't have Labor Day, Columbus Day, Veterans Day, Thanksgiving or even Election Day to provide a buffer between the waning days of summer and the frantic festivities of the Christmas season.

This holiday drought stretches over so many weeks that they arbitrarily made up a bank holiday just so they could get a three-day weekend during the summer. It's on the final weekend in August and is called, appropriately enough, August Bank Holiday. This situation fairly cries out for another holiday at the beginning of summer, say, in early July. I mean, if they're going to borrow our holidays, they might be better off with one that guarantees a day off and plugs up the gap.

I'd even be willing to trade May Day for it.

The Postman Only Rings Twice

It's a work day, but am I in the office doing those sorts of things I do while I am gainfully employed? Or am I at least out on an errand, enjoying the fresh air and performing a worthwhile task? No, I am sitting at home, in my bathrobe, unable to leave or even take a shower, because I am waiting for a package to be delivered.

The first time I was introduced to this quaint custom was upon our return from a two-week vacation. The very next day, when we came home from work, we found a card stuck to our door admonishing us for being out while a deliveryman had tried to leave a package. Why they couldn't simply leave it in the cupboard beside the door like all the postmen do, I can't imagine, but I suspect it's how they inject a bit of life into their otherwise soul-crushingly boring jobs.

The card, by the way, contained no useful clues—no name, no phone number, no tracking number—even though there were boxes for all this information (but surely that's all part of the game); it merely guaranteed they would attempt delivery again the next day, while we were both at work.

The second notice, again, stated the obvious; "We were here, you weren't. No package for you!" This card contained their promise to not attempt another delivery and assured me they would return the package to its origin if I did not retrieve it within two weeks. It also contained a web address, so I looked it up. (The fact that I would have been completely stuffed if they had attempted delivery during our vacation, or if I didn't have Internet access, was not lost on me as it seemed to be on them.)

Their website contained a number. I called it. It was busy. I called again. It was still busy.

For the next three days I called the number, sometimes for stretches of an hour at a time, and never got through. With the clock ticking, I returned to their website and dug through the site index for any helpful information. All I found was a second number, buried deeply within the "Contact Us" page hierarchy. This second number put me in touch with a computer and a forty five minute quiz. After three attempts at shouting inane answers into the phone, the computer capitulated and agreed to mail my package to a local Post Office, where I could pick it up, at my convenience, for a fee.

At least I knew the location and business hours of the Post Office so, after paying the ransom, I lugged my prize home. The only satisfaction I received was the knowledge that the deliveryman had had to hump the heavy box up and down two flights of stairs, twice. It was small compensation, and from then on I lived in fear of another delivery. It was sure to happen; the Christmas season was approaching and that means packages, lots of them.

My fears were realized last Friday. Ironically, my wife and I had taken the day off from work to celebrate Thanksgiving. We were home all morning. At 11:30, we stepped out of our flat to do some shopping. At 11:33 (yes, that's the time written on the card) the deliveryman struck. I can't be certain what lengths these guys will go through to brighten up their day but I don't discount the notion of them hiding around the corner in the hope of catching you out.

Unlike the other, this note contained a tracking code, as well as a phone number with a live person on the other end. "These people," I innocently thought, "understand customer service." What I couldn't have guessed at the time was that they simply enjoyed frustrating you in person.

I explained to the woman that a delivery had been attempted and asked how I could get the package.

"They'll deliver it Monday." Of course! Everyone in Britain is independently wealthy or related to the Royal Family or both and do not require the inconvenience of employment.

"And what will happen when I'm not here?"

"They'll send it back." She said this as if it made perfect sense, her tone implying it would be my fault should this occur.

"What are my other options?"

"You can pick it up here." "Here" was a fair distance away, but it seemed the only course of action.

"All right, I happen to be free right now; I'll be there in an hour or so."

"Oh, you can't pick it up today."

"Why not?"

"The package is still on the truck, isn't it?" she said.

"Bloody hell!" I said, and hung up.

This is why I'm sitting here, wasting a day's vacation time, unable to go out or step into the shower for fear the doorbell will ring and my last chance at getting this package will be lost.

And the most depressing thing is, it's not even December yet.

Money

I have some issues to discuss vis-à-vis being an American in Britain, about our cultural differences and how the previous two hundred years shaped and molded them into what they are today, but that sounds like a lot of work for me and, frankly, a boring result for you, so I'll just tell you how I came to buy a new wallet instead.

For as long as I can remember, I have been carrying a money clip. The reason for this isn't because I had too much money to fit in my wallet, or that I liked to flash big wads of cash around; quite the opposite. Much of my life (more of it than I care to admit) was characterized by having very little money, and the few greenbacks I had never hung around long enough to justify taking my wallet out of my pocket, so I got into the habit of stuffing my folding money into the front pocket of my jeans.

In later years, when I acquired a bit more dosh, this habit resulted in a disorganized jumble of bills so, to keep them orderly, I smoothed them out and fastened them together with a large paper clip. I no doubt would have continued using this frugal innovation, for it suited me well and paper clips were easy to come by, except that I received an actual money clip for Christmas one year, and that was that.

From then on, I always, only carried my bills in a money clip. Even in America this is not a common practice, but the few who remarked on it seemed to think it was classy. For the most part, however, it wasn't even noted and I never thought much about it.

The money clip transferred to the UK without a great deal of trouble. I simply traded in my greenbacks for the multi-sized, multi-colored UK bills and life went on much as before. Until I happened across a fine and educational book entitled *Guide to Pub Life*, which illuminated the cultural issues I alluded to earlier. Apparently, I'm not blending in with the native population as well as I had thought. Even after all this time, certain aspects of my socio-economic upbringing continue to brand me as an American. One of them is the way I handle money.

Back in the States, pulling a money clip out of one's pockets, peeling off a bill and laying it on the bar doesn't draw any undue attention except, perhaps, from enterprising pickpockets. The size of your wad in America roughly equates to, well, the size of your wad.

Money is power. Money is status. It may be a bit gauche to flaunt it in an obvious way (wearing fur-lined capes and pinkie rings sporting diamonds the size of Chiclets is still considered tacky in most social circles outside of Las Vegas), but no one goes through any pains to hide it, either. "A round of drinks for the bar!" "Let me buy you a drink!" "Keep the change!" They all say the same thing: "I have money, lots of it!"

In Britain, money is vulgar, and that's something my American, Capitalist brain has a very hard time getting around. You don't pull out a bill and lay it on the bar here; you pay the barman, he gives you the change and you put it in your pocket. All of it. You don't tip him. Near as I can figure, saying "Keep the change" is like saying, "I don't need this little bit of money, but you do, why don't you keep it." It's an insult, and therefore frowned upon.

Even buying someone a drink is difficult. You can't just say, "Let me buy you a drink," because it implies money is involved. Even the seemingly innocuous, "Can I get you a drink?" has the implication of a favor being bestowed and is best to be avoided. What's more acceptable is: "And one for yourself?"

I'm not really opposed to sticking out as a foreigner; I stubbornly cling to my American pronunciations (I'm surely not going to try anything as daft as attempting to talk like these people) but I have no desire to be vulgar, or to offend, and I certainly don't want to add to the image of the ugly American.

So, while out shopping one weekend—and with an eye toward making a clean break from this old and ingrained habit—I bought a new wallet, tossed out my old one and retired my money clip. Now I no longer feel self-conscious when I buy drinks in a pub; holding a wallet is perfectly acceptable whereas exposing your money-clip is something a brash, and certainly less attractive, American would do.

Now all I have to do is remember to stop saying, "Keep the change."

Temporary Bachelor

My wife is currently enjoying a stay in a local resort, also known as the East Surrey Hospital. Don't panic, she's doing all right, and my plans to write another scathing article about the NHS have been dampened by the pleasantness and competence of the staff. (The NHS is still a national disgrace, but they do have some very nice people working for them.)

Thanks to the limitations of physics, while she's in there, she is not here, and I suddenly find myself, for the first time since setting foot on these shores, unsupervised in Britain. It's been a few years since I've been on my own but the old, bad habits are quickly taking over—you know, staying up past my bedtime, visiting dodgy websites, running with scissors. I think men in general, and myself in particular, aren't capable of doing anything really constructive unless someone is keeping an eye on them. Left on our own, we're more likely to engage in too much drinking, too much smoking and too much trashy television than, for example, tidying up, doing the laundry or Spackling over that hole you made in the ceiling when you went up in the loft to get the Christmas decorations three years ago.

But the activity I am finding the most joy in, is being a slacker where closing doors is concerned.

My wife is a door-closer. Whenever we go out, she closes all the doors to all the rooms in the flat. Just in case.

Now, the bathroom door I can agree with. You never know when the toilet is going to explode, sending searing shards of porcelain projectiles through the front wall and into the courtyard, but I can't imagine anything spontaneously combusting in the bedrooms.

My wife always counters with logic that only she can understand.

"If there is a fire, a closed door can give you an extra ten minutes to get out."

"But we're already out. If there's a fire, we won't be here!"

"It's still a good idea."

So the doors remain closed all day while we're at work, and all evening if we go out. But, reckless scamp that I am, I leave the doors open when the flat is empty. I wonder if this allows the laundry—which by now should be taking on a life of its own—to run riot through the hall and into the living room, perhaps stopping off at the kitchen for a sandwich along the way.

Despite the guilty pleasure I feel in exercising this power, I do harbor a dark fear that I'll come home some evening to a smoking ruin where our block of flats used to be. The firemen will be wandering around packing away hoses and ladders and all of my neighbors will be standing, forlorn and desolate, in the courtyard, their accusing eyes upon me as the head fireman explains the situation:

"We would have been able to save the building but somebody left their doors open and the fire spread too quickly. You wouldn't have any idea who that might be, would you?"

Maybe, on my way up to Surrey this evening, I'll swing by the flat and close all the doors. Just in case.

Bank Holiday Britain

We went to the National Portrait Gallery in London yesterday. At least that's what my wife calls it. I call it "A building filled with paintings of people I don't know drawn by people I've never heard of." It was, despite this, a good day out, and served as the focal point of our effort to enjoy the last Bank Holiday until Christmas.

We get eight paid holidays per year in Britain, the least of any EU country. In the States I got 13 holidays, along with 19 vacation days, 12 days sick leave and five personal days. Tallied up, that's 49 days a year I didn't have to go to work. If you compare that to the 25 vacation days and eight bank holidays I get in England, you might think I received the short end of the deal but in practice—thanks to the "use it or lose it" vacation policy they have here—I take a lot more vacations now than I ever did in the US.

But I do miss those long weekends.

This was a typical British Bank Holiday in all respects, bar one—it was clear, sunny and warm. Otherwise, the motorways were jammed and the sea sides were heaving, which was why we decided to go to London instead of Brighton.

Seeing as how it was a Bank Holiday—a day when a lot of people were traveling—our train journey to London involved a lot of buses. The reason for this is they were working on the line. This is one of those annoying necessities that come along on a seasonal basis, like the annual road works on the Interstates, which happen in the summertime when a lot more people are on the roads. I can't fault them for this; Lord knows the tracks need fixing up and, while you're bound to upset a few people no matter when you do it, you're generally better off not messing around with the commuter rush hour, something that the Interstate work crews never seemed to catch on to.

So we made it to London, which was, in a relative sense, deserted. On a normal day, you spend much of your time jostling tourists out of your way, as well as being jostled out of the way by locals. On this day, it was possible to walk down the pavements unimpeded. The only time I have ever seen the streets this deserted was after 9-11, when all the American tourists vanished. Today, happily, it was simply because

14

everyone who lives in London was at the seaside. This became obvious as the day progressed and I found that the vast majority of overheard conversations were in languages I couldn't understand spoken by people with puzzled expressions consulting tourist maps.

We bought a picnic lunch of sandwiches, crisps and beverages for £7.29 at a corner convenience store and dined in St James Park, surrounded by trees, greenery and the aforementioned bewildered tourists. It was peaceful and serene, the only annoyance being the beggars. These were of the four-pawed and web-footed variety—ducks on the dole and unemployed rats sporting furry tails—and I kept a wary eye on them while eating in case they decided to organize and bushwhack us. Nearby, I saw a sign exhorting us to not feed the pelicans, which I took to be a joke until I saw one, later in the day, eyeing up a woman eating a sandwich.

In all honesty, sign or no sign, it would never have occurred to me to approach one of these creatures and hand him anything. They are as big and fearsome as a surly chav; put a hoodie, sunglasses and some bling on this bird and you wouldn't be surprised to find people handing their wallets over to him. As we walked away, he was still coolly appraising the woman, perhaps wondering if he should kill her first before robbing her.

The National Gallery is in Trafalgar Square, which was inexplicably packed. We toured the portrait gallery and then the public galleries where there are pictures of boats and trees and an occasional nude. At length, culturally sated, we capped off our visit in the National Gallery café, where we paid £11.58 for scones and two cups of tea. Hell-o tourists, welcome to London; give us all your money.

It was, on the whole, a grand day. But that was yesterday; today I'm on the bus on my way to work. I see it's shaping up to be another sunny summer day, which is sadly irrelevant at this point.

sigh

Just 118 days until the next Bank Holiday.

Prague

Thursday, Travel:

I'm relaxing in a café in Prague after a long and hectic day, with a cigar in one hand, a good Czech beer in the other and my long-suffering wife doodling in a Sudoku book at my side. Like most travel days, this one has left me breathless and awed by how far away from home one can get in a relatively short time. Also typical of travel days, it began ungodly early.

Don't they make holidays that begin at 10:30 in the morning? Why can't you lie-in on your first day off from work instead of having to jump up to the alarm and stumble over suitcases while fumbling for the light switch?

To answer my own question, the reason is the three-hours-early rule for international travel. So, even though our flight wasn't until 11 o'clock, we were obliged to be at the airport by 8, which means catching the 7 o'clock train, which means leaving the house by 6:30, and so on. All so we can sit in a shopping mall for three hours watching as our flight creeps slowly up the departures board. I'm sure this rule was conceived by the airport retailers' association. No one else benefits from having all these people milling around with no place to go and nothing to do for the better part of three hours.

Our journey began, as all of ours do, on foot. Whether we are heading across the street or across the ocean, we generally start out the same way—walking up the Bishopric toward the town centre. This lends a sense of adventure and possibility to even the most casual outing; when you step outside your door, you never really know where you are going to end up. On this day, we ended up in Prague; the day before, I ended up in Hampshire and the day before that, in T K Maxx. Like I said, you never know.

Our hotel is conveniently located on the cusp of the old city and a block away from Wenceslas Square and the major shopping district. Preliminary reconnaissance revealed we are just down the street from the Powder Tower, which, being nearly 200 feet in height, serves as a comforting homing beacon.

The Powder Tower was constructed in 1475—years before Columbus got the urge to visit China—and is so named because its purpose was to store gunpowder. It's an impressive structure, even by today's standards and must have held a massive amount of explosives; I can only imagine what that did to local property values.

My initial impression of Prague is a manageable, friendly place of cobbled streets and impossibly old and beautiful architecture. This is the city centre I am talking about; greater Prague is a sprawling, traffic-snarled metropolis, much like any other European city I have visited, with the exception that the suburbs—possibly the most unattractive I have ever seen—still suffer from Communist-era construction programs. Row upon row of cheerless, squat, grey blocks of concrete blight the landscape everywhere you look. They are so soul-suckingly dreary that is it not hard to appreciate how living in one would make you want to wear stodgy, black garments and wrap a kerchief around your head.

But somehow the heart of the city survived the occupation and remains a showcase for medieval architecture—though now it is engaged in a new life-or-death struggle against the forces of capitalism. During our casual stroll we found ample opportunities to part with our money; if you're looking for unbelievably ugly amber jewelry at bargain prices, Prague is the place to be.

And the prices in Prague are a bargain, though it takes some mental gymnastics to work that out. Czech Crowns (Kč) come 38.16 to the Pound so a horribly tacky necklace made of what looks like orangeish billiard balls on a string with a 1,070 Kč price tag is a real steal when you figure that is just about £28. At least while you are admiring it in the window. By the time you pay for it, that may have changed; the Pound to Crown ratio recalculates hourly. For the purposes of mathematical convenience, therefore, we are using a static figure of 40 Crowns to the Pound so I don't get a headache every time I need to convert something.

One thing that did surprise me when making mental calculations as to the true value of merchandise is that I no longer think in terms of dollars. I never thought of an item as being worth X number of pounds, which makes it really worth so many dollars. I guess that was inevitable, but I'm still not sure how I feel about it.

Just to cap off the idea that we were in bargain-hunters' heaven, we stopped for dinner at one of the many local restaurants. I had a starter and we ordered a nice bottle of Pinot Grigio. After our entrées we ordered dessert and coffee. I also had a shot of the local beverage. All of this came to around £27 (or $44); it would easily have been twice that in Horsham.

My introduction to the local moonshine is worth noting. When we ordered coffee, the waiter asked my wife if she wanted schnapps to go along with it. She declined, but as I like schnapps, I asked if I could have one. To my surprise, our heretofore obsequious waiter said, "No." Then he explained that schnapps is a lady's drink; men drink Slivovice. I knew I was in trouble when he presented the clear liquid to me in a tall, thin shot glass that had apparently been stored in liquid oxygen, then waited expectantly for me to sample it. I took a sip and managed to smile at him. Even with its taste dulled by the extreme cold, Slivovice is what my wife calls a "rough" drink. And when I say rough, I mean you would need a belt-sander and a blowtorch to blunt the sharp edges. The waiter, satisfied I was enjoying the local hospitality, disappeared into the kitchen, whereupon I dumped the remainder into the dregs of my wine glass and gulped my coffee to get the taste out of my mouth.

Slivovice is pronounced SLIV ah vitz; remember the name so you don't accidentally order it.

Friday, Walkabout:

Friday was sunny and we took the opportunity to explore the city centre, plot our future excursions and check out the shopping district.

I highly recommend a trip to Prague, but do it soon. They have shrugged off fifty years of communist oppression at a frightening pace and rampant capitalism is now making it indistinguishable from many other European tourist destinations. EU regulations will, no doubt, finish the job.

The shopping district has a McDonald's density I have previously only experienced in Buffalo, New York, and they apparently build one KFC franchise for every resident family group. The avenues are lined with Marks & Spencer's, H&M, TGI Friday's, Coca Cola billboards and even Tesco's; the only thing that kept me from mistaking it for Croydon was the relatively light traffic and a welcomed absence of Starbucks outlets.

We left the hive of burgeoning capitalism for the old town square—the geographic hub of the old city—and a chance to marvel at the stunning architecture. The Staroměstské Náměstí, as the locals know it, is fabulous and reminiscent of the Grott Market in Brussels. Grott Market is also easier to pronounce, so that's how I'm referring to it throughout our stay. It's an attractive destination and made a convenient reference point, as all of the attractions we were interested in were only a short walk away.

For the most part, walking is easy in the historic district. The cobbled streets are narrow and winding and not frequented by vehicles. The only drawback is, the cars and trucks that do navigate them, do so with a frightening alacrity, their drivers apparently convinced that everyone will jump out of their way. They fairly zip through pedestrian crossings without a thought or backward glance to see if they've left any bodies in their wake. I never noticed any mishaps, but there is a conspicuous lack of older people shuffling around. Perhaps this is how they deal with their old age pensions crisis.

Despite the chill weather, the streets remain lively with tourists and buskers. The Charles Bridge is lined with street vendors and the crowds rival those of a summer day on Westminster Bridge. Our guidebook observes that, in the height of the tourist season, you can't cross the Vltava River without a catapult.

Also lining the bridge, and stationed at key points among the more popular tourist attractions, are beggars. They are not as obvious or pushy as most I have encountered. Here, custom seems to require them to kneel as if in prayer and lean forward on their elbows, holding out a cup or their hat for passersby to toss coins into. I'm sure it has something to do with it being a Catholic country. At any rate, it looks an uncomfortable way to make a living.

Saturday, Storming the Castle:

At breakfast the second morning it occurred to me I was learning more about how northern Europeans live while on holiday than I was about how the local Pragulodites go about their everyday lives.

I used to be keen on researching how the locals lived, but this involves dedicated drinking sessions and long, drunken conversations in out of the way and, more often than not, dodgy bars. On my more recent trips, being older and, more to the point, married, I tend to see the insides of museums and historic buildings more often than drinking establishments. While this might serve to keep me out of foreign jails, it does mean I have to look harder for interesting anecdotes. I suppose I should be happy for the trade-off; at my age, sleeping on a park bench isn't the lark it used to be.

And so, refreshed from a sober night in a proper bed, but lacking anything interesting to say, we took a morning meander through the Grott Market on our way to Prague castle, and managed to catch the Astronomical Clock in performance mode. Every hour on the hour, for the past 516 years, the clock chimes and images of the saints perform a morality play. Compared to, say, *The Matrix*, it was a bit of a disappointment. A series of puppet-like images peeked out of some windows, then disappeared. The action was wholly unsatisfying and, if there was a plot, I missed it. In the interest of fairness, I should point out that this was constructed in the days before MTV, Xbox and iPods, so it was probably thrilling to watch when it was first unveiled.

The castle, I am relieved to report, was not a disappointment. It isn't so much of a castle as it is a complex of impressive and diverse structures surrounded by a fortified wall. It still dominates the city and serves as the seat of government for the Czech Republic. It's also the city's main tourist attraction.

Most prominent is the massive cathedral dating back to 1344. Several hundred years in the making, it rises spectacularly toward the heavens and still has the power to impress. What impressed me most was how bloody cold it was inside (though, with ceilings that high, it must be a bitch to heat); I could only sympathize with the countless generations of Slavs who congregated there for hours at a stretch, getting frost-bitten knees from enforced praying on the frigid concrete floor.

Like most churches, the interior was brooding and sober, but the windows were sure pretty.

Elsewhere, the complex was a mixture of old buildings that you could go into and newer ones (presumably with central heating) that you could not. That these latter buildings housed an active government was highlighted by the changing of the guard ceremony at noon. The guards' outfits—a hybrid of medieval garb and chunky, communist fashion—are a perfect match for the self-conscious pomp, circumstance and marshal music that make up the ceremony itself, which involved a lot of arm swinging, foot stomping, displays of weaponry and music that sounded like a cross between *The Man From U.N.C.L.E* theme song and *Thunderbirds*.

Dinner that evening consisted of two entrées, a bottle of wine, desserts and coffees and cost twenty quid. Eat your hearts out.

After dinner, as we meandered back toward the hotel, we encountered one of the local beggars who, having finished his shift, was wandering around the streets talking to himself as homeless people are wont to do. There seemed nothing remarkable about him and we passed by without much notice.

Around the next corner, two buskers were setting up under an archway. They tuned up their violins and began playing Vivaldi, using the archway's acoustic properties to mimic the sound of a full orchestra. It was thrilling to listen to.

Then the beggar wandered by. He stopped just beyond the small crowd that had gathered, listened for a few moments, and then began singing along. He wasn't in danger of winning *The X-Factor*, but it was, nonetheless, unexpectedly competent. I've rarely encountered such talent in a vagabond before. He sang for a while, then shuffled off, presumably to spend his hard-earned charity on some Slivovice to ease the aching in his knees.

Sunday, The Snows of Staroměstské Náměstí:

The Czech people may have embraced western fast-food franchises and retail outlets, but they still have a thing or two to learn about capitalism. At Prague Castle—their most popular attraction—finding out where to part with your money for the privilege of enjoying the exhibits was no simple matter. And on this morning, it was made even more difficult by the addition of over a foot of snow.

Actually, I'm glad it snowed. I've been thinking, against my better judgment, about taking my wife to Upstate New York during the winter so she can see what a *real* winter is like. Now I don't have to. We woke in the morning to find mountains of the white stuff piled outside of our hotel with plenty more drifting down from the sky.

It was all the good things I remember about snow; white, fluffy, fun to walk in and incredibly pretty. The streets were hushed due to the thickening blanket and the fat flakes floated like feathers through the grey dawn. And best of all, I knew I was leaving it behind the next day.

Despite the snow, we made a full day of it. When you're on holiday, you can't let a little thing like a blizzard stand in your way, and everyone else seemed to feel the same.

We toured the old Jewish Synagogues, had lunch and walked, once again, over the Charles Bridge. Tourists, buskers, beggars and merchants were all there, oblivious to the cold and snow.

Dinner that evening was even cheaper than the night before. Our waiter brought the bill, went over each item with us, showed me the total and then pointed out the service charge that I could pay, if I felt the service was worthwhile. The service charge came to about a pound, which, in my opinion, is more of an insult than a tip, so I left him a bit more.

As we gathered our survival gear and suited up for our return to the snow-strewn streets, he returned to our table and tried to give the extra money back. He couldn't seem to grasp why we had given him more and we had to convince him to take it. When we left the restaurant, he met me at the door, shook my hand and wished me a good night. All for a four pound tip.

Monday, Blue Skies, Sunshine and Cold as a Well-Digger's Arse:

I'm sitting in the same café I started out in, with a cigar in one hand, a good Czech beer in the other and my long-suffering wife doodling in a Sudoku book at my side. This time we're waiting for our mini-bus to take us back to the airport where we will catch a plane to take us back to the grey, damp British weather.

I can't wait.

Today the sky is brilliant blue in a way I haven't seen in years; not, in fact, since I was last in America enduring another grueling winter.

The weather enhanced the sightseeing (with the emphasis on "sight") and we took the tour of the town center and Charles Bridge, braving the sharp cold in coats meant to keep out the damp more than the chill. But now we're warming up in the café and watching the Czech version of Big Brother on a TV mounted to the wall. It looks as inane as anything the Brits could come up with and drives home the point that, during our entire stay, I never once attempted to speak a word of Czech. I really didn't have to; everyone spoke at least some English, all the signs were in English and, if I had attempted to, I'm sure I would have found it impossible. Czech, being Slavic in origin, isn't as easy on the tongue as the romance languages.

Despite (or perhaps, due to) the weather, Prague was a better than average holiday. The season kept the crowds manageable and the occasionally inhospitable climate provided a bit of nostalgia as well as a chance to introduce my wife to a New York-style winter without actually having to spend another February in Albany. Our guidebook tells us that mid-summer in Prague—when uncomfortable levels of heat and humidity are the norm—is not popular with the tourists, either. Maybe we should arrange a return visit in July so I can reacquaint myself with even more reasons why I don't miss the weather in my erstwhile home, especially if they get mosquitoes and black flies.

The Perennial Losers

As envisaged, following close behind the expected American World Cup defeat, came the anticipated loss of the England team. But unlike the American team, whose wins and losses went largely unnoticed in their home country, England struggled to stave off defeat before the eyes of the entire nation.

Well, almost. I didn't watch The Game, nor did my wife, and most of the people at the Crawley Folk Festival (which was where we were when The Game was on) didn't appear to know or care about what was transpiring on a playing pitch in Germany, either. The folk festival provided a few blissful hours where I felt like I was among normal people—even though some of those people were decked out in jingle bells and whacking at each other with sticks. Otherwise, every waking moment was all about The Game: What are you doing on The Day? Where are you planning to watch it? What do you think of England's chances? Radio stations even had a tongue-in-cheek (I think) excuse line for people who had commitments on The Day (poorly timed weddings or unexpectedly being tapped as pall bearer for your mother's funeral, for instance) to help get them to The Game because that's where God intended them to be. For one hundred and eighty-seven solid days, or, at least, that's what it feels like, there has been nothing you could watch, read, eat, drink, listen to or fornicate with that didn't focus on, or remind you about, The Game. Conversation became decidedly one-dimensional and I began to long for a good old fashioned chat about the weather.

You have to give the English credit for maintaining such ebullience in the shadow of assured defeat. It's the same sort of nationalist optimism that encouraged them to leap from the relative safety of the trenches and run headlong into machine-gun fire. Their childlike faith is so touching I had to confess to an acquaintance in the pub that I wasn't sure if I wanted England to win or lose. I didn't fancy another week of intensified football-mania if they won, but they were so eager for victory I didn't think I could bear to see their hopes so harshly crushed. My companion waved his hand dismissively. "Don't worry, we're used to it."

They should be. Aside from a single contest forty years ago when they beat Germany—and about which they still taunt them ("Two World Wars, One World Cup!")—England hasn't even captured runner-up status in the quest for the coveted Cup. And they've never won a European Championship, either. But that doesn't stop them from stationing themselves, by the millions, in front of their television sets to pray, curse, cheer and cajole while their team lurches toward inevitable defeat.

The Game took place on a sunny, Saturday afternoon and, after leaving the "No Cup" sanctuary of the Crawley Folk Festival, my wife and I decided to stop off at one of our favorite restaurants for dinner. We were a little concerned, as it is a popular place and sometimes it can be difficult to get a table. We needn't have worried.

Our first clue came as we drove along the nearly empty highway, which, on your average Saturday, more closely resembles a car park than a thoroughfare. Likewise, the parking lot of the restaurant was empty of all but three cars—the waitress's, the cook's and ours. Walking across the tarmac and entering the restaurant was eerily reminiscent of an old Twilight Zone episode where a couple finds themselves mysteriously transported to a deserted town. Inside, the dining area was devoid of customers, and the cook and the waitress were in the kitchen. Watching The Game.

We had no trouble finding a seat and dined in solitary silence in the usually crowded restaurant. Even so, when I ordered, the waitress asked for our table number, as if she would have trouble locating us.

After the meal, we drove toward home, over quiet roads, listening to the radio to see how The Game was going. (As in the US during the World Series, even non-fans get caught up, if only out of curiosity, after a while.) The Game wasn't going well at all; they ended up losing in a penalty shoot-out when two overtime periods failed to break the 0-0 tie (which is about as anti-climatic as deciding the winner of a long and bloody war by tossing a coin).

This happened when we were about three miles from home. Almost immediately, cars appeared on the road, and by the time we entered the village, crowds of fans were in the streets, shouting and drinking and blocking traffic and generally being a bloody nuisance.

And I know what they were angry about; now that it's all over, what the hell are we supposed to do with all these England flags and red and white bunting?

I Am Not a Tourist

I'm in London, I've got a rucksack, a camera and an American accent; what I need is a shirt proclaiming, "I am NOT a tourist"

We're on our way to the Royal Academy to see an art exhibit we heard about on a BBC 2 programme. This isn't something your average tourist would attempt—finding their way to Tower Bridge is difficult enough for them, so locating the Royal Academy (or even knowing it exists) is surely beyond their ken.

Frankly, it's at the very edge of our combined abilities, as well. My wife has been there before, but it was long ago so she only has a vague idea of where it is. I'm with the tourists; I didn't even know it existed until she told me about it.

Our best bet, it seems, is to find Buckingham Palace, cross Green Park and then, Bob's your uncle. The only glitch is, we're taking an unfamiliar route through the city and are unsure how to get to Buckingham Palace. I volunteered to walk up to a random Londoner and, in a brash, American voice, ask, "Can you tell me how to get to the Queen's house?" but my wife vetoed the idea on the grounds that, even if she hid around the corner while I did it, someone still might figure out she is with me. In the end, we just followed the tourists.

I had suggested this day for our visit because it is the day of the penultimate (which means "the second to the last"—the Brits like this word for some reason, probably for the same reason they like to say words like "fortnight") World Cup match. London would be more easily navigated, I reasoned, with everyone at home watching the telly. What I failed to take into account was the staggering number of tourists. Also, on the route we are taking, we would be unlikely to encounter any actual Londoners even on a normal day; the locals are not as keen on Royal gawking as we Americans, and the types of people who attend art exhibits aren't generally distracted by such things as the most important sporting event in the known universe.

I've visited Buckingham Palace before, but usually we approach via The Mall. This time we're coming up the road bordering the 42-acre Palace Gardens—fittingly called

Buckingham Palace Road—and past the Royal Mews where the Queen keeps her horses and golden carriage (we all need a place to keep our golden carriage, don't we?). Just beyond the mews and around the corner from the Ambassador's court stands the Victoria memorial and about 100,000 tourists.

It's breathtaking to see the number of people who want to visit the Queen's house and catch a glimpse of the changing of the guard. (I've never seen it, myself, but my guess is one guard comes out and takes the place of the guard on duty so he can go off for a wee and a pint of bitter.) Judging from the size of the crowd, the Royal Family have nothing to worry about—if the British ever dissolve the Monarchy, they could just go to America. We love the Royals, and would certainly welcome them. This would also provide the advantage of enabling us to fawn over them without requiring travel to the UK where we have to put up with funny money and dodgy breakfast meats for the privilege.

Also popular with the Americans is the Official Buckingham Palace Gift Shoppe. Filled with all manner of regal tat, it's almost as well-visited as the guard replacement ceremony and is certainly more convenient as it's open all day. Naturally, I had to go in to gape and smirk, along with my fellow countrypersons, at the souvenir crowns and Buckingham Palace Biscuits while secretly wishing I had the nerve to buy one. I may live here, but I still love this stuff.

So forget what I said when I started this rant; I guess I am a tourist after all.

We're Number Two

E ven I am astonished by the power of the printed word.

After my previous book was published containing a chapter about how Horsham has been getting an undeserved drubbing as a terrible place to live ("We're Number One," page 131), a new poll was released by Channel Four wherein my adopted town ranks as the second best place in all of the UK to put down roots.

While I remain surprised by the number of people who rallied to Horsham's defense due to my book (that must have been the reason, don't you think?) I am in no way shocked by the outcome. Horsham is, as I have always maintained, a nice place to live. The only place nicer is Winchester, city of the famous cathedral that failed to ring its bells when someone's baby left town, or so the song says.

Horsham is populated by polite people who earn a good living; people who, when they walk past you on the street, quietly mind their own business and rarely ever try to slit your throat with a broken beer bottle and set fire to you just so they can steal your mobile phone. This is good news, indeed, for my wife, whose original home—Hackney in central London—ranked dead last in the same poll (dead being the operative word; there is actually a street in her old neighborhood dubbed by the locals as 'murder mile'). Good thing she had the sense to leave when she was three.

Horsham has low unemployment, low taxes and no homeless people wandering around hitting you up for a few coppers when all you want to do is get to the end of the high street so you can enjoy a walk in the park. It is also one of the sunniest places in Britain and enjoys, along with the rest of the southeast, mild winters and relatively bug free summers.

On the downside, the general lack of excitement was mentioned (as if that's a bad thing), along with overcrowding and expensive housing. And what do wealthy, bored people do with themselves? Mostly, it seems, they eat: one in five Horsham residents is overweight. No wonder I feel so at home here.

And Horsham is interesting, in its own way. At least three or four times a year I am surprised by the unexpected appearance of carnival rides, flaming baton jugglers, people on stilts dressed up as giant flies or hordes of men prancing around with jingle bells strapped to their ankles while whacking at each other with big sticks. Having the option of walking out your front door and finding a giant slide not ten minutes away is quite gratifying. I've never actually gone down the slide, mind, but the opportunity is there if I ever decide I want to. Can you say the same about your town?

But don't take my word for it, come over for a visit, we can always use the tourist dollars. Just don't get any ideas about moving here—it's already too crowded. Go to Winchester instead; I hear it's nicer.

Thanksgiving

Complaining is easy; complaining creatively with liberal sprinklings of humor and/or sarcasm is a bit harder, but still not all that difficult. Saying something positive, yet funny, is a challenge, and one that I am not up to this early in the day. So I am going to put aside my usual serving of hilarity (you do find these chapters hilarious, don't you?) and simply tell you about my Thanksgiving.

I love Thanksgiving, and I really enjoy celebrating it in England because it causes such confusion in those around me. Everyone has heard about Thanksgiving, but not a lot of people outside of North America (don't forget, our Canadian neighbors celebrate it, too) really get it. Just the idea of having a holiday that doesn't celebrate winning a war or fails to imbue an ancient pagan ritual with artificial Christianity is enough to cause wonder in most Europeans. While many can admire the idea of a special day set aside for gathering with the family to have a big meal and ruminate on the good things in our lives, the majority fail to grasp the significance and near reverence attributed to the occasion by those of us fortunate enough to have grown up with the tradition.

Visit any town or city in North America on Thanksgiving Day (except for New York City, where the famous Macy's Day Parade is held), go to Main Street and you will see…nothing. That's because everyone is inside, with their families observing whatever tradition it is their family observes on this day. There will be a hush all around you and the unmistakable feeling that something significant is happening. It's a lot like Christmas Day, only without the forced merriment, drunken parties and the ever-present sound of Slade singing, "Here it is, Merry Christmas."

The best thing about Thanksgiving is that it is a non-denominational holiday; it may have been started by Christians, but anyone can join in. It doesn't demand adherence to any set of beliefs, it doesn't require you to be a member of any organization or nationality, and you don't have to drag a tree into your house or send cards to people you haven't seen in ten years. So even over here (or, perhaps, especially over here) I make a point of observing The Day.

This Thanksgiving—having, in years past, fallen short in my efforts aimed at recreating a traditional American meal—I decided to go native. We had our own, private dinner made entirely from ingredients we could find locally instead of importing items from the States. And it was grand. The Paxo stuffing, the Bisto Gravy dust, the turkey joint (just try to fit a full-sized turkey into our oven) and the up-market cranberry sauce were all delicious. I'm not sure if this means the UK is becoming more like the US, or that I've been here so long I've become accustomed to the strange cuisine but, either way, I was not disappointed.

I am happy to report that only three swear words were required during the preparation of the meal and they were all used at once, when I dropped the pumpkin pie while putting it in the oven.

This, of course, all happened on Sunday; I was in Birmingham on the real Thanksgiving Day, working on a particularly recalcitrant installation while everyone in my native country was having the day off. We didn't leave the site until 9 PM. I checked into my hotel—a Premier Motor Inn on a nearby industrial estate—and went to the bar/restaurant for a chicken curry. That was my Thanksgiving dinner. When I got back to my solitary room, I had nothing to do but look forward to another long day, so I went to bed. And then I had the type of experience journalists probably dread: an event so perfectly timed and serendipitously placed that it sounds contrived. I dreamed I was riding on a train through London, looking over the night time skyline, at the glowing dome of St. Paul's Cathedral, the lights of Tower Bridge and the illuminated spokes of the London Eye, and a sudden feeling of joy and gratitude swept over me as I realized how blessed I was to live here.

I'll spare you the details, and point out only that it prompted me to expand upon the theme in my waking hours, and to devote a portion of our Thanksgiving meal to sharing my mental checklist of Things I Am Thankful For with my wife (and then putting her on the spot by making her come up with her own list without the benefit of preparation). But I am thankful, and grateful, and it's nice to have a day devoted to remembering that.

So I hope you all had a wonderful Thanksgiving and that you have as many things to be thankful for as I do.

Now get your ass up to the attic and pull out those decorations; Christmas is here.

Holiday Spirit

Something truly unusual happened this past weekend; I was able to give my barber a Christmas tip.

Sheer happenstance, as it turns out; if I had stopped in a little earlier or a little later, a total stranger would have cut my hair. Instead, I ended up with the same barber who has cut my hair at least three times in a row—the one who always sits me down and asks, "What can I do for you?" and I have to avoid responding with something ironic like, "world peace and a gin and tonic" or the screamingly obvious, "Cut my hair." But this has made him memorable and earned him a couple extra quid, which I would not have given to the other guy. Cutting my hair one time does not give you the right to expect a Christmas bonus.

This got me thinking: I haven't handed out many Christmas tips since moving to England. Time was, I knew my paperboy and my mailman, I had a regular barber and, believe it or not, a maid. All of these people got a little something extra around the holidays. It was a nice tradition, and one I would willingly continue if only I could.

What stops me is the fact that, since moving here, I have not met my paperboy, I have no idea who my mail carrier is (and if I did track him down, giving him a tip would not be the first thing on my mind) and there seems to be some sort of law about commoners hiring domestic staff. This is not an indictment of British society but more of a comment on our modern way of life.

In our quest for convenience and instant gratification we have shoved aside social interaction. Chitchat with the butcher takes time, and hearing about his daughter's new baby or telling him how your son is doing at college doesn't increase your net worth. In fact, going to the butcher in the first place is a waste of time, which is why there are so few butchers and why most of us pick up our meat in shrink-wrapped packages from a nameless teenager working behind the deli counter in Sainsbury's.

Our modern culture seems to promote anonymity and discourage continuity. The shops in our town come and go with alarming frequency. The aforementioned barbershop I have been patronizing for the past year and a half has changed hands three times, and it is not unusual to find an entirely new staff each time I visit. My bus drivers are familiar enough, but there are a baker's dozen of them and they rotate on a daily basis. Should I tip them all or just the guy who happens to drive me home on Christmas Eve? And do you actually tip bus drivers? I never had one in the States, and I can't image anyone in England would expect a tip.

For familiarity and continuity, you can't beat your local pub, but even they are not exempt. You might stop into your favorite pub for a pint and banter with the bartender only to find the comforting oak interior has been stripped and replaced with pine paneling and the inglenook fireplace converted to house a plasma TV. And when you return the following week, it will be a Bistro.

Everything is done for me by people I never see. The lawns are mowed, the hallways cleaned (not very often, I might add) by people who sneak in and out unseen, the various shops I frequent are staffed by recent high-school graduates who are there one day and gone the next and I have yet to see the same doctor. All this leaves me nostalgic for a familiar face and a hand to shake and say, "Thanks for everything, have a Merry Christmas!" and resulted in me tipping a barber I have only seen four times.

I think the world is a sadder and lonelier place for it, but it does save a lot of money.

Happy Birthday

Very soon now, certainly by the time you read this, I will—against my better judgment—have turned another year older. That's not such a bad thing, really, especially when you consider the alternative. But, historically, birthdays have not exactly been kind to me.

Now, I'm not implying that anyone has the right to expect their birthday to be the highpoint of their year, but I wouldn't mind if it wasn't the annual nadir. During my childhood, my birthday generally coincided with the storm of the decade, or was the day I came down with a near-fatal dose of Bulgarian Measles or Nepalese flu. My 21st birthday—something every American looks forward to as a watershed event—was so gut-wrenchingly nightmarish it is still keeping my therapist's children in Reeboks. My 30th and 40th birthdays were at least unappalling enough that I can't remember a thing about them (or, perhaps, I just blacked them out), and the only event of note to take place on my 50th was the morning phone call telling us my wife's grandfather had died. Not exactly something to inspire an outpouring of mirth.

At my age, I really don't care about my birthday; I just want it to go by unnoticed. True, it's nice to get a few cards or, as I did last year, an e-mail from my son telling me to call him so he could wish me a happy birthday on my (international) dime. But aside from those niceties, it's best to ignore it. In Britain, I have discovered, this is not allowed.

Back in the States, I could go to the office on my birthday secure in the knowledge that no one would take a blind bit of notice. In fact, no one would even know. And if a particularly close friend happened to remember, it would probably only result in a drink at TGI Friday's after work, with him paying. Here, I'm expected to provide cakes, candies and assorted treats for everyone in my office. It's required by an act of Parliament (well, that's what I was told) so no one is allowed to let their special day slip by without providing a party for everyone whose birthday it isn't.

This means I have to give my birthday a lot more thought than I am used to. I've been thinking about it for weeks: what sort of treats to provide, what sort of quantity (and quality), when I'm going to buy it and how I plan to get it all there. Since I ride the bus, dragging in 5 carrier bags of cakes, pastries and assorted chocolates is no easy feat. It's also a lot to ask of a person who, truth be told, they barely speak to for the other 364 days of the year.

I do not reveal these things lightly; I was afraid it might jinx an already jinxed day, making it that much worse. But this morning, I received a letter informing me that a long-awaited hospital appointment has been scheduled for, yep, my birthday.

So now, in addition to schlepping all the materials for an office party around with me, I also have to spend the better part of the morning in the loving arms of the NHS. That has to mean the day can't get any worse and, after spending a few hours in the local hospital, it will probably be the best birthday I've had, or will have, for years.

All Things British

A group of us made our yearly pilgrimage to the Pantomime last weekend. I won't bother explaining what that is—if you're British, you already know, and if you're American, it will take more words than I have available to provide you with even a glimmer of understanding. Suffice it to say it is an essential ingredient of British life and, due to the alarming decline in boarding school enrolment, plays an increasingly important part in maintaining the tradition of gender-role confusion among young Britons.

Late January isn't exactly Panto Season. But you Brits already know that, or at least, you should; which was why I was surprised at the absence of Pantomime-related questions on The Test.

I'm referring, in case you haven't guessed yet, to the *Life in the UK* test, a multiple-guess exercise required of all applicants wishing to become UK citizens (and soon, of anyone planning on stopping in for a while). In a few years, this island will be swarming with people who know the number of seats in the Welsh Assembly, the percentage of women in the work force and how many countries are in the Commonwealth, but nothing at all about British life.

Don't get me wrong, I do not object to the idea of the test in the least. If I owned a country, I'd want people planning to live there to put in a little effort; you know, find out a few things about the place and maybe learn the language. If you want to be an American, be prepared to take weeks worth of classes, sit an exam or two and swear an oath that they will expect you to take very, very seriously.

Perhaps this is why I don't mind the naturalization process as much as many home-grown Brits seem to think I should. Standing at attention every morning, with my hand over my heart, and swearing to the flag, God and country was good preparation for swearing allegiance to the Queen. I would have far more reservations if I simply walked into the country and was told, "Make yourself at home. Here's the address of the benefits office and a complementary map of our transportation, power and defense infrastructures."

Taking up citizenship should not be done lightly; attaching a bit of pomp and ceremony helps give it a feeling of significance. And the test, as long as you have a minimal grasp of the English language and read the book, is impossible to fail.

The only issue I have is that they should ask more relevant questions. If it were up to me, I'd pull out the section on the economic ramifications of Britain joining the EU and stick in a couple of questions on actual, real life in the UK. Such as:

1. If someone offers you a Glasgow Kiss you should:
A) Pucker up
B) Duck
C) Tell them you don't swing that way
D) Then duck
E) And run

2) Prince Philip:
A) Is King of Britain
B) Once asked an indigenous Australian business man, "Do you still throw spears at each other?"
C) Is a doddering old man who wandered into Windsor Castle and won't leave
D) Was the mastermind behind the plot to kill Princess Diana (NOTE: D will be accepted as a correct answer only if you produce proof of your subscription to *The Daily Mail*)

3) You're at a Pantomime and a shapely woman walks on stage wearing thigh-high leather boots with spiked heels, fishnet stockings and a shockingly short tunic. This character is pretending to be:
A) A transvestite
B) A slapper
C) A boy
D) Julian Clary on a typical Saturday night

4) Haggis is eaten:
A) Only on Burns Night
B) By Royal Decree, every Sunday in Scotland
C) Mostly on a dare
D) Never. It's a joke the Scots play on tourists

5) A train is scheduled to leave Redhill at 9:47 and arrive in Croydon at 10:15. When would be a prudent time to arrive at the station?

A) 11:00

B) 9:30 so you can be on time to catch the 8:05 to be in Croydon at 11:20

C) Don't bother. Take a taxi.

D) Don't bother. Stay at home and watch Eastenders

6) You are officially in The North when you cross:

A) The Scottish Border

B) The outskirts of Birmingham

C) The Watford Gap

D) The Thames

7) Cocking and Lickfold

A) Are words one does not use in polite company

B) Cost a tenner downtown

C) Are villages in Sussex

D) Were outlawed in Victorian times

8) The London Eye is

A) A private detective agency

B) The Big Brother logo

C) A glorified Ferris wheel

D) A euphemism for 'Anus'

9) You see a group of men running at breakneck speed down a steep hill chasing large wheels of cheese. The most likely reason for this is:

A) They are engaging in the poor man's version of running with the bulls

B) They really like cheese

C) They are participating in a time honored sport

D) The cheese is incidental; they are simply trying to get to the pub before last orders

10) You know you've been in Britain too long when

A) You are able to make up a test about it

B) You think it's funny

C) You friends in America wonder why you think it's funny because it's clearly gibberish and you have almost certainly lost your mind

D) All of the above

Answers: 1. D&E, 2. B or D, 3 thru 9. C, 10. D

.

Adventures in Travel

5:49 AM, Horsham to Dorking:

This morning, I'm on my way to Birmingham. It's a little longer than my normal commute to Brighton but generally no more onerous; I get up at the same time and arrive at my destination around 9:30, which is only an hour and a half later than usual. Over all, it's a pleasant ride through fetching countryside, a welcome change to my normal routine and challenging enough to lend a sense of purpose to the day.

8:52 AM, Reading to Birmingham:

Did I say challenging? What was I thinking? This sort of challenge doesn't instill a sense of purpose so much as it creates an atmosphere of futility.

The train from Dorking to Guildford, as trains in Britain have a habit of doing, failed to show up. Not that I was aware of this; I just thought it was late (no surprise there) and hopped on what I thought was the overdue 6:25 to Guildford but which turned out to be "the train that stops at every backwater, inbred little village in Surrey before rolling into the Guildford station twenty minutes after the 6:51 to Birmingham has departed," or something like that.

Being new to this sort of thing, I resorted to my standard Plan B: panic. As soon as we slowed down I bounded off the train, raced to the ticket office and explained my predicament. Give them their due, they were sympathetic, and instructed me to go to Reading to catch the 8:10. There was a train leaving for Reading now on platform 8; I could catch it if I hurried.

So I sprinted back to the platforms and, just as the doors were closing, jumped back on the train I had just gotten off of. Turns out, I was going to be afforded the opportunity of visiting every remaining backwater, inbred little village in Surrey—and parts of Berkshire—that I hadn't had the privilege of seeing while the train was making me late for my first connection.

Surrey, by the way, is lovely. If you every find yourself with nothing in your appointment diary, you could do worse than catch this train and take in all the bucolic scenery and twee little towns. If, however, you are late for work, I suggest you drive, and start early. As it was, I found myself an unwilling passenger aboard a train that wove an erratic path toward Reading, arriving just in time for me to miss the 8:10 to Birmingham by, oh, about 20 minutes.

Fortunately, another panicked visit to the ticket office confirmed there was also an 8:40 to Birmingham. After some confusion, the train was located and I am now rolling happily and swiftly—and in a more-or-less straight line—northward.

Well, maybe not so happily. I haven't been able to grab any breakfast in all this confusion and the snack car is too far away for me to want to leave my stuff behind, and if I take it all with me someone will probably steal my seat which maybe wouldn't be so bad because there is this guy sitting behind me jabbering into his mobile phone as if he's coaching a rugby match long distance and he just will not SHUT THE HELL UP!!!

It's okay; I strangled him. And stole his coffee. I feel better now.

4:25 PM, Anonymous Pub, Birmingham New Street Station:
This pub really does have a name but I'm too lazy to get up, step out the door and read it. I ducked in here strictly for some food (tuna with mayo and sweet corn on a toasted bun) because I'm hungry and it's close to my platform. But that's about the only thing that recommends it. A train station bar is pretty much like an airport bar: the food is mediocre, the beer expensive and everyone is from somewhere else and too busy fiddling with crackberries, texting on mobile phones or talking to themselves with Bluetooth headsets sticking out of their ears to be personable.

This morning, incredibly, I made it to Birmingham in time to stop on my way out of the station to pick up some breakfast and a bottle of water. With the carrier bag of groceries in one hand and my briefcase in the other, I headed for the taxi rank.

The queue was only a quarter mile long when I arrived, which wasn't a bad thing as it gave me plenty of time to study local taxi etiquette. Ideally, a taxi would pull up, the lucky traveler would hop in and they would speed off. If the occupied taxi was delayed by traffic, another empty cab would pull up behind it, allowing the next person in line to walk down to meet it.

As you've guessed, my taxi was held up (no, no, not with a gun; I know this is Birmingham but, really). So I walked down the line and reached for the door handle of my cab. At the same time, the cab in front drove away. My cab pulled forward and I

41

had to snatch my hand back. When the driver saw this, he stopped, so I reached for the door handle again. But he thought I had moved away and started forward again. We did this dance for about nine yards while everyone in the queue looked on. When I finally got the door open, I managed to catch my shopping bag on the door handle, allowing me to fall gracelessly into the back of the cab and pull the door closed on my foot.

As I struggled to disengage my shopping and my foot, I realized the driver was speaking and I couldn't understand a word he said. He was of Indian extraction, but it wasn't an Asian accent that had me confused, it was his Birmingham accent. That seemed only fair; he couldn't understand me, either, nor did he know the address I wanted him to take me to. After much hand gesturing and pointing at maps, I eventually ended up where I wanted to be, but he may have given me the grand tour of Birmingham and several outlying districts along the way. How am I to know?

Unbelievably, after all of this, I encountered that rarest of creatures: a good day at work. The meeting was uncharacteristically productive, I was confident in what I was doing and we hit every item on the agenda with time to spare, which meant I had to hang around downtown Birmingham to wait for my train home.

Birmingham center is actually quite nice. I understand it used to be grim but they've rebuilt much of it and it now has a modern, airy, posing-for-the-tourists look. Trendy shops abound, there are restaurants and bistros a-plenty, and cafés, you betcha, but what I couldn't find was a decent pub. A man could die of thirst there. I was on my third, ever-widening circuit around Victoria Square before I happened upon The Wellington, a traditional real-ale pub, where I spent an enjoyable hour before retreating to my current location in the Anti-Pub.

The Wellington had so many ales on tap they were listed on what I mistook to be an Arrivals/Departures board, which told me I've been spending too much time in train terminals. I ordered half a pint of number 14 and received a full pint instead.

But I'm used to this; my accent makes "half a pint" sound like "have a pint" to British ears so I'm always ending up with more beer than I ordered. It's a burden, but somehow I manage to put up with it.

Besides, after a morning like I had, I think I deserve a full pint. Several, in fact.

Fuerteventura

A slightly tongue-in-cheek adventure

Saturday, Mostly Waiting:

This time, we're on our way to Fuerteventura. Yeah, I didn't know where it was, either.

Fuerteventura, I am told, is one of the Canary Islands, which serve as a sort of Caribbean Paradise for the UK—a quick place to hop to for clear skies, sandy beaches, tropical fun of all types and the opportunity to meet time-share salesmen. But that only tells you what island group Fuerteventura belongs to, not where they are. Typically, I had no idea; I thought they were near the Bahamas but it turns out the Canary Islands are just 67 miles off the coast of Morocco. As such, they are irrelevant to most Americans and, with the Caribbean Islands warmer, closer and boasting better beaches, I doubt I am going to run into any of my countrymen once we arrive.

This is a Travel Day, which means waiting: waiting to leave, waiting for the train, waiting in a succession of lines at the airport, waiting in the departure lounge, waiting in the boarding lounge and then waiting on the plane. We spent ten hours traveling today and only during four of them were we actually moving anywhere.

I made good use of the down time by coming up with a list of ways to liven up a boring flight:

- Listen carefully to the safety instructions and, at the appropriate moment, slap your forehead and say, "So that's how those seat belts work!"

- Remind those around you that, if the oxygen supply should fail, the masks falling from the ceiling are simply meant to distract you while you suffocate and die.

- If there is a queue for the toilet, join the end of it, tap the guy in front of you on the shoulder and whisper, "I've got the primer, are you the one with the detonator?"

Sunday Morning, Coming to Terms:

The most convenient thing about Fuerteventura so far is the weather. Although a climate Mecca for Brits, temps in the seventies, to me, are merely comfortable. But this allows me to wear a jacket, which provides storage space for my camera and cigar paraphernalia.

Our chosen accommodation is suitably located close to the centre of town, allowing us easy access to beaches, shopping, restaurants and, should we desire it, public transportation. Unfortunately, it is also more chronologically challenged than many of the other tourist compounds scattered about the island and therefore contains some, shall we say, surprises.

First of all, we are in an apartment that sleeps four but, because there are only two of us, we had to pay extra for "under occupancy." I had never heard of this before and I have to say it rankled me a bit, especially when I saw the place: it might be called spacious, but only if your idea of spacious is cozying up with your roommates. Granted, there is an adequate living room/kitchen/dining area, a double bedroom, a good sized bathroom and a suitable balcony furnished with flimsy plastic chairs and a tiny, unusable table, but I am hard-pressed trying to come up with three other people I would choose to spend seven days in such confined quarters with. I do not now, nor have I ever, had friends I was that close to, and when you consider having to deal with toothpaste tubes left open, wet towels draped around the bathroom, dirty clothing heaped in the corners and empty beer cans cluttering up every flat surface, the extra fee begins to sound like a bargain.

Additionally, in getting ready for our first day of this tourist extravaganza, I found the shower brace broken and the showerhead hanging down, pointing at the wall. Later, I found out that, while the showerhead was spraying at the wall instead of on me, most of the water ran onto the bathroom floor.

An impressive mirror is affixed to the wall above the sink but, with no exhaust fan, it is impossible to see anything in it, and when I went to wipe it down it swung violently from side to side. I managed to keep it on the wall but I think I'll use the mirror in the bedroom from here on.

Otherwise, the place is clean and tasteful in a "furnishings by Cargo circa 1996" sort of way. The mattress is as comfortable as a prison bunk and signs of casual workmanship and the unfortunate effects of settling abound.

Still, and I must stress this, it's pleasant. Despite the constant breeze, the weather is agreeable, the food options are plentiful and cheap and the pool below is big, blue and inviting. You really could do worse for the money.

This morning, we need to forage for supplies. My wife just got up. I recommended she take a bath but now she's saying there is no way she's going to take a bath with her knees tucked under her chin in that diminutive excuse for a tub. I guess I'd better go see if I can fix the shower bracket.

Sunday Afternoon, Surveying the Domain:
I'm sitting on the balcony enjoying (surprise, surprise) a tasty beverage, nice Cuban cigar and an interesting view of the pool area. The beaches, I understand, are clothing-optional and, from the look of things, no one much cares what you don't wear while sunbathing around the pool, either. This isn't really as impressive as it sounds; most of the clientele at this place are old, overweight, or otherwise in possession of the type of body that makes you glad clothing was invented. And, yes, I include myself in that group, which is why I'm up here looking down instead of down there in the altogether searing an unforgettable image on the corneas of unsuspecting onlookers.

We had a lovely stroll through the town and along the local beach today. For a manufactured community, it's a bustling little place. Mostly it's filled with restaurants, clubs, bars, and whatnot shops designed to part the tourists from their Euros.

Since we'll be dining out a lot, we checked a random sample of nearby restaurants. Originally, we'd planned to cook a few meals in our apartment but some of the other "surprises" we discovered while trying to prepare a simple lunch were the two burners, microwave and toaster they expect you prepare meals with and the cunning manner in which they hid the sink beneath the hot water heater. This place is advertised as "self-catering," but they obviously don't expect you to do much cooking.

Nor should you; the local fare is agreeably tasty and inexpensive so it really would be a shame to stay in the apartment to eat beans on toast. When you look at a menu, you think, "Wow, that's cheap." and then when you realize the prices are in Euros, not pounds, you think, "Wow, that's really cheap!" On our first evening, we had a tapas meal of grilled sardines and Canarian potatoes with wine, and were feeling quite continental until we realized what we had ordered was, in effect, posh fish and chips. Still, it only came to around a tenner for the two of us.

It's getting late now. The people down below are starting to get dressed and drift back to their rooms. Time to chill out for a bit before hitting the streets in search of dinner.

Monday, The Island:
We took the two-dollar Coach Tour (or the 1.50 Euro tour if you prefer) of Fuerteventura today. I like coach tours because someone else does all the driving, they provide a bit of local color and they make me feel young. I should think the first two reasons would be enough to convince people from any historical epoch to join in, but the average person on a coach tour always seems to be able to remember what they were doing on Armistice Day.

We toured the entire island from Corralejo in the northern tip to the famous beaches of Costa Calma in the south. We saw the east coast, the west coast and took a harrowing ride down the mountainous spine of the island.   Fuerteventura, which unsurprisingly translates to "Great Wind," rose from the ocean during a series of volcanic eruptions some 30 million years ago and nothing much has happened here since. The most used phrase throughout the tour was, "There is nothing of interest here."

A Frenchman, Jean de Bethencourt, conquered the Canaries, and Fuerteventura along with them, for the Spanish in 1402. He landed with 40 soldiers and the island, then populated by around 1000 cave dwellers, promptly and wisely surrendered. It's been in European hands ever since, despite its proximity to Africa.

The people, until about 200 years ago, subsisted on agriculture, but then the climate changed (without the help of our carbon footprint) turning Fuerteventura into a virtual desert. Those who couldn't escape to neighboring islands, where rainfall was unaffected, either learned to adapt to the desert climate or starved to death. Today, goat farming is the main occupation of those not making a living fleecing tourists.

Fuerteventura became a tourist haven during the 1960s solely due to its climate. It's a relatively stable 70-80 degrees year-round and it rarely rains. On the other hand, apart from the man-made beaches and artificial oases, the landscape has all the bucolic charm of a strip mine. The valleys are straight out of *The High Chaparral* and the mountains more resemble slagheaps with names.

There are 29,000 year-round residents on Fuerteventura, which is less than the town of Horsham. But add to that about

89,000 tourists and you'll understand why the water and electrical systems are so over-stressed. One might think, with wind and sun in abundance here, alternate forms of energy would be the answer, but that technology is expensive and fuel here is cheap so the power station and water filtering plants both run on diesel.

Being a desert, water is a constant problem. We heard on the tour that drinking water is shipped in. The tap water comes from the desalinization plants and is then collected and recycled for crops. The locals don't even drink the tap water, something that is really handy to know up front.

Despite all this, people flock to Fuerteventura to visit and to live, which has led to a hodge-podge of manic and often ill-conceived construction. All along the tour route we encountered mammoth resorts either left half-finished due to bankruptcies or completed, yet abandoned, due to apathy. Housing, too, is subject to these vagaries. With so many people wanting to live here, whole communities are built to house them, but then they sit, empty as ghost towns, glutting a market where—contrary to the laws of supply and demand—house prices continue to rise.

The government of Fuerteventura is about the same as any other. A famous local artist constructed a stainless steel mobile, which the government purchased at great cost and erected in the only location on Fuerteventura where there is never any wind. When it didn't twist and twirl as advertised, they tore it down and put it back up again—in the same location. We saw it today; it still doesn't move.

But there is bounteous wind out here on our balcony, I can tell you. It seems to be getting stronger and it makes having a cup of coffee and a cigar a bit of a challenge. Time to call it off and go find some dinner.

Tuesday (very early) Morning, Living Up to Its Name:
This wind just never stops! It is so strong now that the cheaply hung door keeps clacking as the pressure pulls and pushes it, serenading us with a constant clunk, clunk, clunk and removing the option of sleep.

We were gamely attempting to ignore it but then I got up to go to the loo and managed to run face-first into a concrete wall when I thought I was returning to the bedroom. My exclamation of surprise ("Oh my, who put this wall here?" or something like that) woke up my wife, and probably everyone else in the compound, so now we're both sitting in the living room, listening to the clunk, clunk, clunk of the door, staring bleary-

47

eyed into space and trying not to blame each other for not being able to sleep.

I think, once again, it's time to put my limited DIY skills to use.

Tuesday (later that same) Morning, The Calm Before the Storm:

Currently, the showerhead is propped up with some crumpled carrier bags, the garbage bin is jammed in place with a dustpan and brush and the door is wedged closed with a bit of folded cardboard. I have to wonder what else I'm going to have to jerry-rig before the week is out.

At least we were able to sleep. Last night, my wife discovered that the couch is more comfortable than the beds but we didn't feel like tossing for it so we both returned to our prison cots after I stabilized the door. From here on, however, we may take turns sleeping on the couch just to get a restful night.

By the way, when I said, "Beds," I did mean two. Even though this accommodation is for a couple, there are two single beds bolted to a common headboard with a night stand between them, eliminating the possibility of pushing them together if you desire. I find that rather puritanical for a place that encourages you to swim naked.

The wind, if anything, is even stronger this morning, and it has brought with it a cloud cover, which makes it even cooler. Still, if you can find a place out of the wind that the sun can reach when it peeks between the clouds, it's quite mild. But such places are hard to come by.

I notice no one is at the pool. Small wonder. This would be a good day for the intrepid bather, as you could snag a good seat, or—more to the point—any seat you wanted. Neither of us, I am ashamed to say, feels quite so intrepid.

Tuesday Afternoon, True Brit:

The wind and clouds remain but a few brave souls—some dressed in long pants and shirts but others, incredibly, in thong bikinis—have gathered around the pool so we decided, since we were here and since there were ample seats available, we should go down and join them. I put on my shorts so I wouldn't look like a wimp. My wife was smarter; she brought a shawl and is wearing a cardigan. Maybe, if I ask nice, she'll let me borrow her shawl.

The wind has found us, even here at the base of the apartment corral. And it's a strong wind; cushions are blowing away, the pool has surf, but everyone is remaining gamely in their spot because they're British.

When they go on holiday, no matter what the weather, Brits sit by the water with their newspapers, towels and sunscreen, wearing shorts and ridiculous hats, encouraging their children to play in the raging sea or rippling pool because that's what Britons on holiday do, they enjoy themselves, grimly and with dogged determination. But I'm not British, and I am therefore not grimly enjoying myself. I'm just cold.

Tuesday Evening, Beating the Odds:

Turns out, my wife was cold, too, so we went back upstairs. It was too cold for the bikini babes, as well. They abandoned the pool shortly before we did and I noticed no one was lounging topless.

We're currently sitting in the living room with the balcony door closed, watching the weather grow cloudier and windier and, believe it or not, rainier. There are only 24 days of rain on this island per year (and we were told they all take place between November and February) and we managed to hit one of them.

How lucky can we be?

Wednesday Morning, Dark Clouds and Silver Linings:

It's cool and windy this morning but there is some sun and the promise of warmer weather. And at least it's not raining.

I had my first semi-decent night's sleep since I got here. With the drop in temperature, it was cool enough to be comfortable and with the door not banging all night long I was actually able to fall asleep.

During a nocturnal trip to the loo, I met my first cockroach—a friendly fellow who just stood there staring at me and not bothering to run. There was no use in killing him; 10,000 of his relatives would show up for the funeral. I can't fault the hotel for a single, fearless cockroach, but I can fault them for the overall shoddiness of the place. In a way, it's comforting because it's just like being at home. In the tradition of my landlord, the owners of this place do everything—from the furnishing, the carpentry, the appliances, the plumbing, even down to the bedding, toilet paper and soap—with an eye, not toward quality, aesthetics or customer convenience, but toward cheaping out.

This results in an undercurrent of dissatisfaction and knowing, if they tried just a bit harder, our stay would be that much more pleasurable and I wouldn't be spending my time and energy doing daft things like stabilizing the trash bins or wedging the door closed.

Before I'm sued by the Fuerteventura Tourist Board, allow me to point out that some of the apartments here appear to be undergoing renovation, so they are apparently upgrading the place. Although it must be said that I haven't actually seen one of the renovated apartments so I have no idea what they look like; for all I know, they may be overhauling them to bring them up to the level of ours.

Wednesday Noon, Waiting for the Maids:

Despite initial optimism, the clouds thickened, the wind stiffened and the temperature remained stubbornly and decidedly cool. The few hopeful holidaymakers who had earlier installed themselves around the pool have retreated, surrendering to the climate.

If you've booked a holiday for the sole purpose of sitting in the sun, this has got to be a bit of a disappointment. We aren't so keen on the sun and surf but had hoped to relax on the balcony and just read or lounge by the pool and sip cool drinks.

As it is, we're huddled on the couch wrapped in a blanket.

We took a stroll this morning and that about wiped us out. The incessant wind just sucks the warmth—and all your energy along with it—out of you. We came back for some lunch but the maids haven't been here yet. If we start making lunch, they'll be sure to arrive in the middle of it. So all we can do is sit here, trying not to fall asleep. This isn't difficult because, due to the impending arrival of the maids, I removed the wedge holding the door in place and the energetic clunk, clunk, clunk precludes sleep.

All I want is some quiet, a little peace, a place to sit where the wind isn't seeping into my bones and rustling the trees and rattling the door. I want to feel the sun warming me, see the blue sky and hear nothing but the gentle rumble of the distant surf as it lulls me into placid slumber.

But the wind just goes on and on and on and on and on and on and on and the clunk, clunk, clunk, clunk, clunk pounds in my head like a low-level migraine. I'm tired and cold and hungry and I can't even watch the television. There are 29 channels on this thing but only one is in English and it's subtitled in, of all things, Arabic. Right now, it's showing a documentary on the life of John Delorean, and even if I wanted to watch it, the sound doesn't work very well when it's—wait for it—windy. What is wrong with these people? Haven't they figured out yet that it is always windy here? No wonder the first settlers on this island lived in caves; it was the only way to get out of the wind.

Funny how, on the tour, we didn't see any lunatic asylums; there must be a few around somewhere to hold all the people driven crazy by the wind wind wind wind wind...

Wednesday Evening, Atención:

Hola. I am afraid Señor Harling will be not able to update his travelogue for a time. He was found running naked along the sea front screaming, "Stop, just stop! Jesus, Mary and Joseph will you just stop!" We had no choice but to intervene.

We are not objecting to naked people, but we are not allowing to take the name of our Holy Mother in vain and Señor Harling seemed distraught and perhaps a danger to himself or other tourists. He is resting comfortably now, a guest of the Clìnica Mèdica, Turista Loco Ward. His mind is mending nicely and he should be well and able to continue his story mañana.

Carlos Fuentes-Mendoza, Capitán del Policía,
Corralejo, Fuerteventura

Thursday, The Zen of The Wind:

I've had a perfectly peaceful night. There was some confusion yesterday afternoon but the men in the long white coats were very nice and convinced me to go with them in the van. I'm ever so glad I did. They gave me a nice comfy robe and took me to a large room with chairs and tables and lots of other tourists who seemed just as glad for the peace and quiet as I was.

My wife came to visit me later and brought my cigars. I wasn't allowed my lighter or cutter or anything to write with but the kind men in the lab coats escorted me to a smoking room and lit my cigar for me. I met a pipe smoker there and we had a grand time discussing tobacco preparation techniques.

After that, a group of us played rummy without keeping score until dinner was served. Then we were led to our bedrooms. They were white and warm and quiet and the walls and floor were padded with the softest pillows. I slept in the most blissful comfort, without the clanking of the door or the howling of the wind or the cold seeping into my bones.

In the morning I was so refreshed I felt I could return to my apartment but they said I needed to learn the Zen of the Wind first.

I needed to believe in the wind. The wind is my friend; the wind is a giver, not a taker; I should accept the wind around me, connect with my inner wind and become one with the breeze. It would give me life; it would set me free. And more importantly, it would allow them to let me return to my apartment.

I gave it a shot but, really, it was a load of bollocks. Then they gave me a bottle of little blue pills, which improved my attitude a lot more than the Zen mumbo-jumbo they'd been feeding me, so they let me out.

My wife and I had designated Thursday as "the shopping day" so, after a late start, we walked into the center of town and perused the stores.

Shopping is another reason people flock to Fuerteventura. The tax is extremely low here so things like booze, tobacco, electronic goods and jewelry are really cheap. Because the Canaries are sort of EU but really not, there is an official limit on what you can bring back, but the unofficial limit is how much you can stuff into your suitcase and not get caught with.

We enjoyed a late lunch at a charming Bistro on the seafront then retired to our balcony to read and relax in the fresh breeze. When the breeze started getting too fresh for my liking, my wife suggested I take one of the little blue pills and that seems to have worked.

We're down in the pool area now, still in the breeze but with a welcome sun warming us and giving us a bit of color so the folks back home will believe we really went on holiday and didn't spend the week holed up in our flat.

Wouldn't you know it; the clouds have rolled in, just when I was getting comfortable. There goes my chance for some holiday color and, if that wasn't bad enough, I'm getting cold again and the wind is really...

Just had another blue pill. It's still windy and cloudy, but I don't mind.

Friday, Lanzarote:

When we first arrived, we signed up for a tour of Lanzarote, sort of a "two islands for the price of one" deal. It turned out to be a good idea; we've about done all there is to do on Fuerteventura, so Lanzarote provided an interesting diversion.

Lanzarote is Fuerteventura's smaller neighbor to the north and is so close it is clearly visible from our hotel lobby. Lanzarote is just as arid but has a different character and feel to it. First off, in addition to being a desert wasteland, it's also mostly covered in lava.

On 1 September 1730, the ground split open and began spewing vast amounts of magma and hot gases, converting the heretofore peaceful, agrarian island into a virtual moonscape.

The island stabilized in 1736 but burped again for a few months during the 1800s leaving a third of it covered in a thick and craggy layer of volcanic rock and burying the remainder under 18 inches of porous black stones the size of pearl tapioca.

The lava fields still contain hot spots and we were treated to the sight of brush bursting into flame when stuffed into a hole in the ground. We also watched steam shooting from another hole in the ground a few seconds after a guy poured water into it and, as a bonus, were allowed to have stones shoveled from the ground and placed in our hands for about half a second until we all shouted, "Ow!" and dropped them.

The lava fields are now a National Park and are so eerily lifeless and rugged NASA used them for training astronauts in preparations for the moon landings. A local guide told me that the actual moon landings were filmed in the lava fields as well, (you didn't think those men were really on the moon, did you?) and for an extra €50 he showed me the authentic "One Small Step For Man" foot print.

Incredibly, even with the island covered in moon dust, the locals found a way to make a living. Before the catastrophe, wine making was big business. And now, three hundred years later, wine is being made again; though this time the vines have to be grown in holes dug through the lava gravel.

Huge areas of land are pockmarked with indentations sporting a clump of grapevines coiled at the base. If enough of these pockmarks produce large enough vines they can gather enough grapes to make a few vats of sour wine. We were all given a taste when we visited the vineyard. To my knowledge, no one bought a bottle. Still, you have to give these people credit for trying.

Another business that has fallen on hard times is the dye industry. Years ago, the cochineal beetle was used to make red dye. Synthetic coloring has pretty much wiped this type of dye out, as it takes 150,000 crushed beetles to produce 1 kilogram of dye. These days, the beetles are mostly around for the benefit of the tourists; they produce authentic cochineal dye only by special order for people who don't mind paying $587,392 a half ounce.

Camels have been on Lanzarote for some time but, like the cochineal beetle, no longer have any practical use beyond amusing the tourists. But riding the camels is certainly popular among the mildly adventurous; more popular even than beetle viewing, despite the fact that looking at the beetles is cheaper and safer and doesn't smell as bad.

At one point in our travels, we came across a bank of wind turbines. My wife tried to convince me they produced electricity, but I know the truth: they don't run on wind, they generate wind, which Lanzarote exports to Fuerteventura. This has been the major source of income for Lanzarote since the 1960s when the wind currents shifted, leaving Fuerteventura comfortable but unable to live up to its name.

These generators are shut down for maintenance only two, non-contiguous weeks of the year. They are never shut down on the same week twice for fear the tourists will catch on and everyone will book their holiday during the downtime.

I offered the guy €500 if he could arrange to have them shut down for just one day but he said it was out of his hands. Typical; I'm stuck with this wind and short of locking myself in my room and wedging my door closed I'm never going to get any peace until I'm back in Sussex where, at least if it is windy, I can comfort myself with the knowledge that it isn't going to stay windy from now until the end of bleeding eternity...

Guess it's time for one of those little blue pills.

Lanzarote has, if this is possible, even less rainfall than Fuerteventura but they still manage to raise bugs, produce wine and cater to a fair number of tourists. They don't have the sandy beaches and they host only a limited number of resorts, so the amenities aren't as plentiful as on Fuerteventura. Still, if you're looking for a quiet getaway and are not a fan of gentle, but constant, breezes, Lanzarote may be a better choice than Fuerteventura.

Saturday Afternoon, the Last Lunch:

During the single hour my wife and I spent by the pool on Thursday, we—both being of northern European extraction—managed to turn various parts of our anatomy pink and come down with mild cases of sun stroke. Never mind that other people have been sitting in the sun most of the week; we're amateurs, and those other people all have the suppleness of skin normally associated with leather mailbags.

Our overindulgence had the effect of keeping us from enjoying a dinner out that evening, prompting us to, instead, cook eggs on toast in our apartment and retire early. We, therefore, wanted to make our next (and last) night's dinner a bit special so we ordered the Seafood Paella to split between the two of us. Turns out, we could have split it between the two of us and six of our friends and still walked away feeling like we'd made one too many trips through the line at the "All You Can Eat" Buffet.

Consequently, we had a small breakfast this morning, spent some time packing and then went out in search of tourist trinkets. After checking out of our room, we still had three hours before we needed to board our bus to the airport, so we're currently revisiting the charming bistro we found on Thursday.

Today, the day we're leaving, is sunny, warm, cloud-free and, you guessed it, practically windless. I suppose this must be one of the rare days the wind generators on Lanzarote are down for maintenance.

Whatever the reason, the weather today is wonderful. It's warm and pleasant, the beer tastes good, and we're leaving.

Saturday Evening, Going Home in Style:
The airport on Fuerteventura looks like an airplane hangar. It's as if they decided to put an airport here, built a couple of largish hangars and then fitted one out with some seats and Duty Free shops and called it The Departure Lounge.

Since the Canary Islands are not exactly a hotbed of al Qaeda activity, and I didn't see signs of any terrorist separatist groups roaming either Fuerteventura or Lanzarote, I had hopes of being allowed to bring a bottle of water onto the plane with me. I should have known better.

What I was allowed to do was wander around the warehouse-style lounge for an hour or so (they didn't put in enough seats for the amount of traffic that passes through, though this could be a clever ploy to keep people in the shops) until they called our flight. After that, I was allowed to stand in line with 287 other weary and confused passengers as our departure time approached and passed with no sign of an airplane.

Half an hour after our flight was due to leave, a plane pulled up to our gate, as well as to the gate next to ours. This led to a bit of confusion with passengers literally wandering around on the apron trying to find a suitable aircraft to board.

We managed to hit it right on the first try, but when we entered the aircraft, the perky aviation hostess told us to turn left instead of right.

Being so tired and simply glad to sit down, it took us a while to figure out that the seats were, if this is possible on an airliner, comfortable. They were also a lot bigger than we were used to. Naturally, our first thought was that they had made a mistake and would soon be coming for us, telling us to return to the steerage hold.

But, gradually, other passengers began filtering in and soon First Class was about half filled with confused but grateful travelers, all whispering lest the flight crew discover their error and throw them all out.

Turns out (and they freely admitted this to us) that our scheduled plane had been delayed so they were flying us home in a much larger aircraft and, although there was room to spare in economy, they needed to distribute the weight evenly throughout the passenger deck. We weren't being upgraded; we were being used as ballast.

Whatever the reason, it's really nice up here in front of the plane, even if we would be the first to hear the captain say, "Uh oh." Also, seeing as how we're just commoners, we didn't get the full, first class treatment (no champagne in crystal glasses so far), but just sitting in the larger chairs is a welcome change.

I don't know how much first class tickets cost, but I doubt they are worth it just for the legroom. On the other hand, if you're ever offered the chance of upgrading for free, take it.

The Street Where I Live

O ne of the biggest advantages of living in Britain is the outdoor Herfing Season is much longer. (For those of you who are not cigar aficionados, a Herf is when two or more cigar smokers get together for the express purpose of smoking, enjoying, discussing and, quite likely, exchanging and fondling, cigars. I suppose then, the purist would maintain that what I'm doing isn't herfing; having a cigar by yourself and calling it a herf is like saying you have a sex life because you stay at home on Saturday nights to slap Mr. Johnson around.)

The alfresco herfing season, in fact, like the Brighton Pier, never really closes; it just slows down a bit during the winter. This is especially important due to the smoking ban. It is illegal to smoke indoors in the United Kingdom now, as well as in several European counties. And once the EU jumps on the bandwagon, if you want to enjoy a rollie with your pint, you'll have to go to Asia or Africa. I think it's a silly law, but I'm not getting my knickers in a twist over it, not as long as I can nip out onto my balcony for a smoke. And herfing on the balcony instead of at the pub has the extra advantage of keeping me from drinking too much as well as providing an excuse to keep an eye on my neighbors.

From my perch, I have a view of approximately 20 other apartments. I don't make a habit of peeping on them, but if someone walks in front of a window, it's hard to miss it (and here I don't need a telescope like I did back in the US).

The demographic of our little block of flats has undergone a dramatic shift since my arrival. A few years back, the residents hailed from a wide selection of nations, whereas now there is a growing number of Indian families (from India, not the Mohican Sun Casino). Before someone screams "Bigot!" allow me to stress I do not have a problem with this in the least. The Indians are quiet, hard working, friendly and, as near as I can tell, not active members of Al Qaeda, Inc., all qualities I enjoy in a neighbor. So, no, I do not object to them, but I do miss the diversity.

When we first moved in, there were people from all over the world: South Africa, Zimbabwe, Mexico and your lone representative from the US. There was an Englishman with a

Chinese wife, a Dutch woman who used to sunbathe in the nude on her balcony (I still miss her) and, in general, a lot of personality. Now it's mostly young families doing family-type things and minding their own business. It's nice, but not very amusing.

For example, the guy who lived in the ground floor flat beneath us strolled home from the pub one Saturday afternoon wearing nothing but a tee shirt. He unloaded drunken abuse on several of our neighbors (apparently there was some history there), told us all we could kiss his ass (after showing it to us) and moved out the next day. You don't get entertainment like that from people raising toddlers.

And Mr. Loud, although we were pleased to see the back of him, was another unforgettable character.

Mr. Loud lived here for a year or two and in all that time I never once heard him use his "indoor" voice. He had no discernable job and displayed a disturbing disregard for clothing and curtains. The bulk of his time appeared to be taken up with strutting around his apartment in various stages of undress and shouting. He shouted at his wife, he shouted at his child, he shouted at his dog, but mostly, he shouted at people over the phone, and mostly about money they owed him. I expect he was a leg-breaker for a local loan shark or a self-employed telemarketer with anger-management issues. People in neighboring apartments used to close their windows in summer, vainly attempting to keep his F-word soliloquies at bay.

His wife was no slacker, either. One memorable afternoon Mrs. Loud and an unknown woman engaged in some feminine fisticuffs in the parking lot. They drew quite a crowd before their husbands pried them apart.

Next door to our apartment is The Flat Where Nobody Lives. For two years the lights came on every evening and noise from the television seeped through the wall but I never heard a voice nor saw any sign of a human being. I became convinced the lights and TV were on a timer and the flat was empty, serving as a front for some nefarious activity, or at least a tax dodge. During my lighter moments, I suggested to my wife there might be a pair of moldering pensioners slowly decomposing inside while the timers gave the illusion of life and their offspring continued to cash their pension checks.

Recently, the people who didn't live in The Flat Where Nobody Lives moved on (or the rouse was uncovered—no one that I know of ever saw anybody leave the apartment, even feet first) and a normal couple lives there now.

Next door to The Flat Where Nobody Lives is The Man Without Pants—a quiet, middle-aged man who lives alone and always walks around his living room in a pair of orange boxer shorts. Add to this mix an eccentric American who sits on his balcony, in all manner of weather, smoking cigars and typing into something that looks like a keyboard on steroids, and you have to agree this is an interesting place to live.

Or, at least it was.

I think The Man Without Pants is moving. Most likely another family from the subcontinent will move in when he's gone; they'll be quiet and respectful and they'll always dress modestly. Again, I have no objection to this, but it would be refreshing if the person who moved in added to the diversity of the neighborhood instead of blending in so easily.

A nice young lady from Holland, perhaps.

Edinburgh

Introduction:

Just in case you suffer from the same world-geography knowledge-gap as I do, allow me to explain that there are not two separate cities in Scotland, one prominent on the map and pronounced *Edinberg*, and another one, more difficult to pinpoint, and pronounced *Edinboro*. There is, I have discovered after only mild embarrassment, just one: it is spelled *Edinburgh* but unaccountably pronounced *Edinboro*.

Go figure.

Edinburgh is a grey city; grey buildings, grey skies, grey streets. But those are just its physical aspects; the people, the places, the politics—those are very colorful indeed.

We spent our first day becoming acquainted with the city and found it to be tidy, affable and accessible. As with many European cities, all the interesting bits are within walking distance—though in Edinburgh's case you'd better be fit as much of it is up and down steep hills—and anything a daunting distance away can be reached by train or bus.

The architecture is magnificent and the old and the new, if they don't blend together seamlessly, are not as jarringly dissimilar as I have seen in other places. There was, however, one building that stood out.

"That is the ugliest apartment building I have ever seen," I said, as soon as it came into view.

"That's the new Scottish Parliament," my wife said.

It was a marvel to me how any person could ever conceive of a building so magnificently grotesque, much less convince a presumably large group of people to allow it to be built. It appeared to be a cross between a nursing home and a medium-security prison, but built with less care and more revolting colors, by a man with an out of whack spirit level. It wasn't art, I insisted, or bold, or symbolic; it was simply rubbish.

But the Scottish Parliament was not finished with me yet.

The bums, my litmus test for the quality of a city, were fewer than I expected and, in my experience, sat unobtrusively in the background, whereas I would have assumed them to be a bit more vocal. And there may have been fewer of the

60

disenfranchised about than I originally thought as some of the tourist attractions drummed up business by sending young people out dressed in period costume. These costumes were not stylized and sanitized depictions of period dress but often consisted of ragged clothing and, perhaps, a blanket wrapped around the shoulders. Young people dressed like this would wander the crowded streets offering brochures of their particular attraction and I occasionally mistook them for street-people selling the Big Issue.

There are, to no one's surprise, a lot of bagpipers about, especially near the train station and information center where there is a high concentration of tourists. I couldn't help it; I had to stop by for a listen. Bagpipe music still gets to me, and it made me want to go home and get my pipes out. Just think of the money I could make busking in Horsham; I could set up outside of a business and play until they paid me enough to move on.

The Past:

In order to embrace the full scope of Edinburgh, we decided to delve into its past by visiting two historic sites. One was the house and shop of a wealthy merchant, the other the reconstructed tenements of Mary King's Close.

What impressed me about the merchant was that, even though he had it good, he didn't have it that good. Being rich in the 1500s meant two things: more room and more height. The richer you were, the further up in the building you lived and the larger your rooms were. This allowed you more light (while blocking light from those beneath you) and air that wasn't quite as fetid as it was down below. But that's about all you gained; you still had to conduct all your business at street level and, one must suppose, go outside at least occasionally.

For the poorer people (i.e. you and me) life was anything but nice. The pay gap between working class and the upper class may seem large in modern times, but back then, one step down from our well-heeled merchant and his brightly painted quarters had you living in continual twilight, crammed into a windowless hovel with your wife and 15 or so children.

Chimneys were a luxury item, so you and the other 200 families on the Close would cook over an open fire near your doorway so at least some of the smoke would waft outside. Toilets were unheard of so the bucket in the corner made do for the lot of you and every night, when the church bells rang, everyone on the street (and, presumably, the city) would slop the contents of their buckets out the door (while shouting, legend has it, "Garde de l'eau!" or "Watch the water!" which is where the modern term "Loo" is supposedly derived).   The rain of human filth covered the cobbles in an ankle-deep blanket of raw sewage that slid slowly down the streets and slithered into the Loch, which was where the town got its drinking water. (The loch, we were told, soon attained the consistency of gruel.)

The guides did an excellent job of recreating medieval life for us and I wondered if some historians could actually construct an exhibit of an authentic sixteenth century street. I think it would be a marvelous and educational achievement; I also think no one would ever visit it. Hard to imagine anyone parting with nine pounds fifty for the privilege of standing in six inches of shit (and remember, shoes were only for the very wealthy) while waving smoke, flies and plague-fleas off of some rancid meat you are haggling with an old man of twenty-seven over.

Life in medieval Europe was short, brutal and didn't smell so good; so, in the words of our tour guide, "The 1500s sucked, let's go back to the 21st century."

The Present:

We have been planning to visit Edinburgh ever since I arrived in the UK but what ultimately got us up there was a birthday party. My wife's cousin turned (insert round number here) and decided to treat herself to a Posh Do so our first evening found us in formal dress reconnecting with people I haven't seen in years and meeting others for the first time. It was good fun, and I continue to be amazed at being considered one of the family by a room full of men in kilts.

After our tour of the past, we popped into Holyrood Palace, confident it would be open for tours as the Queen was in the US at the time.   They don't allow visitors at Holyrood when the Queen is around lest you stumble across her taking a bath or clipping her toenails.   As palaces go, Holyrood is perfectly adequate; majestic, clean, imposing and conveying the sense that we, as common people, are entirely irrelevant to, and inhabit a world (although not a very important one) different from the ruling class. Basically, it's the same feeling one would expect to receive from a trip to parliament or a nose around Barbara Streisand's mansion.

Meanwhile:

Having glimpsed the backside of the Scottish Parliament, I had to have a peek at the inside, if only for the comic value.

We arrived at the parliament early in the morning along with half a dozen bagpipers and 8,000 runners. It was, we belatedly discovered, the morning of the Great Edinburgh Run and we could do nothing but scrunch up against the building as the swarm of eager runners loped by. Their numbers were impressive, but the main pack soon passed us by and then the stragglers thinned out, leaving us practically alone in front of the strangest building I have ever seen.

Viewing the front of the building was a better experience than my glimpse of the rear, and there was, to my surprise, a sort of grudging majesty about the place. The bamboo poles, I was later told, are actually oak and, although they resemble bars and could conceivably allude to a prison to keep the criminals in or the common folk out, I was assured they hold no significance.

The location of the building, which was as heavily criticized as the structure itself, seemed to make perfect sense. It is across the street from the traditional palace of Holyrood—juxtaposing the past with the present—and at one end of the Royal Mile, which culminates (about a mile away, oddly enough) at Edinburgh Castle.

The Parliament—to continue the controversy theme—was due to open in 2001 at a cost of £40 million, though, in true British fashion (notably the Spinnaker Tower and Wembley Stadium, though you will find others if you make even a small effort), it did not open until October 2004 and only then after a budget overrun of more than 1000%.

The architect, Enric Miralles, died in July 2000, so the world can never know (perhaps by having subjected him to sodium pentothal injections) what was in his mind when he drew up the plans for the building. My theory is, he was a keen practical joker and had a real set of drawings he was preparing to submit along with the "joke" plans he handed over but died before he could reveal the gag.

All that said, the building does grow on you (but then so does athlete's foot). The structure is environmentally friendly and constructed from sustainable materials. Having been built to retain heat in the winter yet remain cool in the summer, there is no need for air-conditioning and most of the heating comes from solar panels.

The public lobby and the Garden lobby are both grand and spectacular spaces. The public lobby, where folks like us can gather to gawp, visit the gift shop or have a cup of coffee, resembles the interior of a mausoleum, while the Garden Lobby—where the day-to-day business of the parliament is conducted—with its interlocking curves of metal and glass, mimics the interior of the Alien mother ship in the aptly named Alien movies.

On a podium near the stairway is a Tracy Emin-esque sculpture of a mountain consisting solely of a rucked up towel and some twigs, though the result is surprisingly and strangely satisfying.

There are a number of committee rooms, which were built to resemble overturned boats, each containing a large, round table and, impressively, a gallery for public viewing. Committees here do not meet in secret.

The debating chamber also has a large public gallery and looks like a cross between a lecture hall and a TV studio, which, I suppose, it is. The stylized microphones at each of 129 member desks bear an unsettling resemblance to hissing snakes and the wall decorations—which are suppose to represent the people of Scotland watching over their elected MPs—can also, without much imagination, be mistaken for whiskey bottles.

Make up your own mind.

Speaking of whiskey, if you visit the gift shop after your tour (and I highly recommend you do), don't miss the opportunity to pick up a bottle of Scottish Parliament Whiskey. If nothing else, that gained them my immediate respect. How can you not support a parliament that brews its own single malt?

In closing, it needs to be said, if you do visit Edinburgh, and you pass by the Scottish Parliament and think, as I did, that it is the biggest waste of space you have ever been unfortunate enough to witness, take the tour. You may change your mind. And if you don't, you will at least come away with some things to think about, and, perhaps, a nice bottle of whiskey.

The Future:

The UK local elections were held just prior to our holiday and, upon arriving in Edinburgh, we found that the Scottish Nationalist Party had gained enough seats to make it the largest party in the Scottish Parliament. They did not gain a majority (or Scotland would have seceded from the UK by now) but their increased presence shows this is a country ripe for revolt.

That the general population is seething with insurrection and a desire to shake off the yoke of English rule was all too apparent, as each interaction with the locals was injected with inflammatory slogans such as, "Can I help you?" or "Are you enjoying your stay?" or "Grand weather we're having; the views from Salisbury Craig should be fantastic."

If this hotbed of revolution heats up, there is no telling where Scotland's future will lead, but as long as they continue to serve a fine dish of haggis and 'neeps, I'm sure they'll do all right.

Full Circle

L
ike a lot of Americans, I defined myself by what my ancestors used to be. I was, therefore, English. And not only was I English, I was a second-generation American, separated from native soil only by my father, who was the first person in my lineage born in the US. This gave me an impressive amount of ancestral cred among my friends who had to climb through several branches of the family tree in order to arrive in Europe.

My ability to talk to someone who was actually born on the far side of the Statue of Liberty did me little good, for my grandfather was a taciturn man who had been a mere boy when my great-grandfather John had bundled his family onto a ship heading west. All I could ever get out of Granddad was the assertion, "Our relatives back in England were horse thieves and they hung them all." While not very informative, it did lend credence to the persistent family legend that John had been deported.

But whatever the circumstances, he left England with his family in tow on the cusp of the 20th century. They became Americans but, like many immigrant descendants, ensuing generations began defining themselves by what their ancestors had left behind. Equally, and like the vast majority of my fellow countrypersons, I never entertained the notion of actually going back there. But as you all know (or should know if you've been paying attention) life can throw a vicious curve-ball at times and, through no fault of my own, I returned to the mother country.

Recently, and even more surprisingly, the mother country accepted me back.

I don't know if this is due to the statute of limitations running out on whatever it was my great-grandfather did, or a terrible clerical error at the Home Office, but yesterday I found myself shaking hands with the Lord Lieutenant (pronounced Lef-tenant) of Brighton and Hove and being warmly welcomed into what is left of the British Empire (and I have to say, they haven't taken very good care of it since Great-Granddad left).

My new status as a citizen of the United Kingdom as well as my continuing member-in-good-standing status in the United

States (yes, despite pervading myths to the contrary, it is possible for American citizens to hold dual nationality) automatically doubles the number of people in the world who despise me and triples the land-area I am supposed to feel responsible for having invaded, stripped of assets and abandoned, leaving the local population to wallow in disease and poverty. Dual nationality is not for wimps, but if my great-grandfather was up for the challenge, I guess I am as well. (I won't be easy. Filling his shoes is sure to be an intimidating task: during his life, he worked in a succession of occupations, crossed the ocean several times—in the days when travel was uncomfortable at best—and, upon settling in America, started his own business, and he supposedly killed a guy in an argument over a cow; compared to him, I'm a right slacker.)

I'm not really sure how I feel about all this yet. It's sort of like getting married; you make a decision that seems like a good idea at the time, then get all caught up in preparations and ceremony only to wake up the next morning with a hangover thinking, "What on earth have I done?"

It's strange to see the rolling green fields, tidy villages and bustling high streets and realize this is now my country, not some foreign land where I am an interloper taking the job of a hard-working, natural-born British citizen. Thanks to my certificate of citizenship from the Home Office, I am now an interloper taking the job of a hard-working, natural-born British citizen *forever*. But, in truth, there is no reason to feel this way; aside from the relatively minor blip of American occupation, I can—thanks to the research of a seventh cousin twice removed in Lancashire—trace an unbroken line of predecessors back to the 1400s, which is more than most Brits can do.

The ceremony itself was a bit disappointing, in that it didn't provide much for me to make fun of. It reminded me of a graduation ceremony for a continuing education class. There was a suitably elegant reception (meaning elegant enough to feel special but not so posh as to put people off), some brief comments that were neither jingoistic nor sentimental, the oath ("I, state your name...," you know the punch line), and the presentations, followed by a chorus of "God Save the Queen" sung by a room full of people who apparently hadn't studied the lyric sheet (and this included the audience).

I was prepared to take the Queen to task for not showing up and, instead, sending a flunky in her place, but the Lord Lieutenant did a marvelous job of pretending to be the Queen. (How does one become a Lord Lieutenant, anyway? I've never seen an ad for one in the local job listings.) Throughout the entire presentation ceremony, she never flagged, and greeted each and every one of us as if she were absolutely delighted to meet us. She had a warm handshake and kind words for every new citizen and posed, with a genuine-looking smile—a skill Tony Blair and Gordon Brown would do well to bone up on—for the official photograph (available for ten quid in the lobby after the show).

After being called, greeted, posed, presented and congratulated, I signed the register and got my party pack, which was the point of all that had preceded this moment. Included among the rest of the bumph—a voter registration form, a nice pen set from the council of Brighton and Hove and a welcoming letter from the Home Secretary (but, conspicuous by its absence, was a greeting from the Queen; I mean, how long does it take to have your secretary whip up a "Welcome to Britain" message and sign it?)—was a UK passport application. It's already filled out and mailed in and, when it arrives, will make a nice addition to my growing collection of UK certifications.

I bet Great-Granddad would be pleased to know one of his descendants is a kindred spirit, a fellow traveler, someone not afraid to face a new life in a strange land. I can hear him now, calling to me from across the years:

"After all the effort, heartache and expense I went through to get us all out of England you turn around and go back! You wanker!"

Seasons

We've just had the perfect summer; perfect, that is, if you are one of those people who enjoy complaining about the weather. And let's face it, over here, that's just about everybody.

After an auspicious spring, summer opened with an uninspiring June, followed by the wettest July on record. August offered us a single weekend of actual, summer-like weather (and you just know someone, somewhere, was complaining about how hot and sunny it was), and then, inexplicably, it was autumn. Every dawn brought grey, wet, miserable weather, and the frigid nights rivaled anything November could have thrown at us. It didn't snow, but it wouldn't have surprised me if it had. Some people even turned their heat on. (Not us, we're too tight; we just bundled up in jumpers and blankets and whined about how cold it was.)

The weather has improved recently, but it no longer matters. We're in the final gasp of August now—Bank Holiday Weekend—which passes for Labor Day weekend in the UK and, likewise, signals the official, if not the technical, end of summer. Any sunny days after this will be classified as "Indian Summer."

The notion of Indian Summer in Britain always tickles me. First of all, it's an American invention and the climate here makes it nearly impossible to meet the official qualifications. Anyone raised in New England knows that Indian Summer refers to a stretch of summer-like days following a hard frost after the autumnal equinox. We occasionally get a hard frost here (known as a hoarfrost) but that mostly only happens in the dead of winter.

Real Indian Summer (or is it Indigenous People's Summer now?) is a grand time, with deep blue skies spanning red and gold dappled vistas. It's a time for apple cider (the non-alcoholic variety), pumpkin pie, apple dumplings and a bowl of steaming raccoon stew (hey, I grew up in the boondocks; we ate whatever we could kill). For me, this time of year always brought with it a deep, almost melancholy, nostalgia, thinking back on the long, seemingly endless, summer days that were now drawing to a close, watching the last of the leaves drift to the brown earth, leaving behind a skeletal landscape, soon to be covered over by winter's icy blanket as the world sank into a deep slumber and waited for spring.

Here, there's no deep slumber; the world just gets tired and cranky and refuses to take a nap. There are no long, snow-bound weekends to devote to jigsaw puzzles, reading or renting half a dozen movies and curling up on the sofa with a cup of hot apple cider (this time with a tot of rum in it). Winter in Sussex means you fasten an extra snap on your waterproof and maybe put on a fleece for your postprandial constitutional.

It's even impossible to enjoy the benefits of my many jumpers; I can't say how often, on a winter's afternoon, I've had to strip off a comfy pullover because it was too warm out. In the States, sweaters were basic winter survival gear, like hot cocoa and Cream of Wheat with brown sugar sprinkled over the top.

All of this is romantic nonsense, of course.

If I never again wake up to three feet of snow that has to be shifted off of my car and out of my driveway so I can get to work, it will be too soon. Snow might be pretty for the first half hour or so, but drizzle doesn't need to be shoveled and green is a perfectly acceptable color for a winter landscape.

Still, if I had the chance, I wouldn't turn down the opportunity of spending another October in New England, amid the blazing trees, the smell of apples and wood-smoke and the perfect miracle that is a true, Indian Summer.

Honest Indigenous People.

It Followed Me Home

Our trip to Dorset, as it turned out, coincided with the annual spider Olympics, heavyweight division. Every time I stepped into the garden I had to snap a branch from a nearby tree and move forward, twirling it in front of me like a foil as if I were fencing an invisible but energetic opponent.

In a way, I was. The spiders, with a few notable exceptions, were not visible during the day but they could collectively spin enough silk over night to trap a fly the size of an Airbus 330. Therefore, every afternoon, the garden table needed de-webbing, as did the chairs—along with a peek under the seats to make sure nothing untoward was hiding there—the pathways and all bushes close enough for a spider to leap from hiding onto any part of my body. (And, as I understand it, your average spider can leap about 50 feet.)

After this daily ritual, I was able to settle in for a relaxing beverage and watch the evening ease over the downs, with only the occasional glance at nearby shrubbery and under the table to make certain nothing unsettling was sneaking up on me.

On Saturday, we left for home.

On Sunday morning I stepped into the spare room and saw the most incredible thing.

Somehow, one of Dorset's mutant spiders had managed to hitch a ride back with us. How this was possible I can only guess; it must have clung to the underside of our car because our suitcases surely weren't large enough to hold it.

Now, I'm going to step out on a limb here and let you in on a little humorist's secret: not everything I write is 100% accurate. No, it's true. This is due to a device we in the business call "comic exaggeration." Though I'm likely to be drummed out of The Society For People Who Think They're Funny for revealing that guarded bit of insider information, I felt it was necessary to gain your trust so you would not doubt me when I tell you that the following sentence is 100% true (after that, you may continue to suspect the occasional hyperbole):

The spider had spun a web with anchor points on the ceiling, both walls and the floor; the business part of the web wasn't much bigger than one of those circular tables you find in

71

bistros or upscale pubs, but the web itself stretched, literally, from wall to wall and floor to ceiling. And there, in the center, waiting patiently for a victim, sat a spider about the size of a Doberman pincer (there's that exaggeration I promised would be coming back.)

The web, like an atomic explosion or an electrical storm viewed from the top of a tree, was a thing of terrifying beauty. It possessed such hideous fascination that, although I was repulsed, I couldn't help gazing at it (this is the same phenomenon that keeps *The X Factor* on the air). It also moved me to consider, for a brief time, allowing the interloper to live.

Upon retreating to the sitting room and mulling it over, however, I changed my mind. The biggest obstacle was how to capture the beast. Any scenario involving a live takedown would require an attack on two fronts and since the spider had made it impossible to get behind the web, it had, in a sense, sealed its own fate. Besides, I felt it would be better that way. Releasing the creature into the wild would only consign it to a life of loneliness, with the other spiders making fun of its west-country accent and taunting it about sleeping with its spider relatives and alleged curious habits with sheep. This might lead the Dorset spider to fight the Sussex spider, which would be too close to one of those old *Godzilla vs Mothra* movies for my taste, especially as I'd be playing the part of the 150,000 terrified Japanese extras.

No, a quick end would be best. Thankfully, I recently bought a Dyson vacuum cleaner with a telescopic wand, which did the trick nicely. I was able to cower in the hallway and extend the wand into the room until the spider, the web and the anchor lines suddenly vanished into the nozzle. Gotta love those Dysons.

I let the vacuum run for another fifteen minutes to make sure the spider was having a really bad time in the cyclone chamber, then stuffed a rag into the nozzle, just in case. The Dyson is now back in our bedroom closet and the world is a safer place, free from the oppressive prospect of an infestation of Dorset/Sussex crossbred spiders.

But still, until I actually empty the vacuum and see the spider-infused debris off with the bin men, I'm going to sleep with one eye open.

Invasion

Britain is being invaded. More correctly, the invasion has already begun, but having secured a stronghold in your capital city, the interloper is now spreading into the surrounding counties, conquering everything and everyone in its wake. Counter attacks are useless. Surrender is inevitable. Resistance, as the Borg are fond of saying, is futile.

At stake is the British way of life, not merely your green and pleasant land, not only your health and happiness, but your famous British reserve, your stoicism in the face of adversity, your stiff upper lip. The peril is so great and so imminent that, if drastic action is not taken soon, you will, in a very short while, be unrecognizable as individuals or as a nation.

I am talking, of course, about Krispy Kreme donuts.

When I heard they were establishing a beachhead in London, I shuddered, feeling, I imagine, as Jean Luc Picard must have felt when re-confronting the aforementioned Borg: we had been sucked in, made one of them and, against all odds, escaped, only to fall into their hands once more.

I first encountered Krispy Kreme in New York City. I was there with a co-worker. He smiled when he told me about this donut shop he had found. He gently led me on, into the shop, so warm, aromatic, inviting. He gave me my first Krispy Kreme (the first one is always free) and smiled as I bit into it.

"These things are like crack," he said.

If it was meant as a warning, it came too late. I was biting into a piece of heaven. So what if each donut contained more calories than six Knickerbocker Glories, three large pizzas with extra cheese and a Whooper with super-sized fries combined, I was hooked, and I knew, whatever the cost, I would be back.

For the moment, Mr. Krispy remained safely at arm's length, and even though I couldn't help visiting the shop on my increasingly frequent trips to New York City, I told myself I wasn't hooked; I could stop at any time. Besides, I was young and resilient; my body could handle the devil in disguise I was dancing with.

A few years later, as luck would have it, I moved to England. I'm not suggesting I left my homeland just to get away from Krispy Kreme but, as a happy collateral effect, it worked a treat.

Fast-forward half a decade. The security I feel in my new home shows its first crack as I read the news: Krispy Kreme is coming. Like the Killer Bees, there is no stopping this migration. The first store opens and slowly, they begin to spread. I tell myself I have nothing to worry about; I'm safe in Sussex, they'll never find me here.

To take my mind off of the looming menace, I give up sugar.

Well, maybe there really was no connection. In fact, I don't recall thinking much about Krispy Kreme at all when I decided to cut down on my sugar intake; I just said that for dramatic effect. Made your pulse race, didn't it?

What really happened was this: I changed my desk at work. I used to sit on the top floor in an office with two other guys. If one of us wanted a cup of coffee or tea, we would ask the other two. I drank about five cups a day, each with one teaspoon of sugar in it.

Then I moved downstairs and found myself in an office full of people who, every time any one of them felt the need for caffeine, they became the "tea bitch" for the entire office. I strongly suspect (and experience proves this out) that the reason behind this isn't the tea or coffee but the desire to spend a restful forty-five minutes away from their desks puttering around in the kitchen area.

Most people don't have a problem with this system; if they've had enough to drink, they pass. But as for myself, if I were a woman, I would be up the duff on a continual basis—I just can't say, "No". So now I'm up to 97 cups of coffee a day, and while I don't mind the havoc 97 daily doses of low-grade amphetamines wreak on my nervous system, I figure my six-pack, which already comes with copious amounts of packaging and bubble wrap, can do without the extra 97 spoons full of sugar.

It's a win-win situation: I can feel virtuous without actually having done anything, and it makes preparing a cup of coffee while queuing up for the 6:57 to Canterbury that much easier.

This, I felt, put me ahead of the game; in my private war against excess calories, I had achieved a victory without suffering any casualties. Then, while visiting a client's office in Guildford, I saw it: a Krispy Kreme Shop.

I'm told that people who live as fugitives, when they hear the knock on the door signaling that their past sins—wearing an off-the-rack suit and a detective's badge—have returned to claim them, mostly feel relieved. In a strange way, this is how I felt; there was no surprise, no joy or horror, simply quiet resignation and surrender to the inescapable. I didn't even pretend to resist. I walked straight in. I bought a dozen.

It's too late for me, but you, as a nation, must resist. Having sallied forth from their London stronghold, Krispy Kreme has spread into Kent, Middlesex, Oxford, Birmingham and the Tesco's Extra in Weybridge. They have breached Essex, Hertfordshire and even Surrey, their staging ground for the assault on West Sussex.

You may think I'm over-stating the danger, but if you don't act now, you will soon find yourself shopping for trousers with a waist size equivalent to the circumference of an oil drum. Do you really want to buy your next rugby shirt from Omar the Tentmaker? Are you ready to give up your thinly disguised moral superiority over Americans and replace it with thinly disguised envy over how slim they are? And consider this: most experts agree that, if everyone in this country gains two or three stone, the island is going to sink.

So please, for the sake of the nation, for the sake of the world, for the sake of your children, resist.

But if you can't, I highly recommend the Apple Crumble.

Stand and Stare, Dammit!

What is this life if full of care
We have no time to stand and stare?
-- William Henry Davies 1871 – 1940

Rushing places seems to be the norm for me lately. No matter how carefully I plan my time, I find myself in a nearly continual frenzy to be somewhere else.

It's not all my fault; the transportation system here seems to be geared to keep commuters on their toes. Currently, I can get to my client's site by two modes of public transportation—bus and train—and both of them require a frantic sprint if I am going to make it.

The bus, depending on traffic, arrives at the town centre bus station (bay 3) anywhere from twenty three to twenty eight minutes past the hour, and my connection leaves bay 17 at twenty five past the hour, ensuring either a mad dash through the crowded bus station—dodging and weaving around less harried commuters like Sarah Palin navigating a pack of animal rights advocates—or an expletive-laced trot to the taxi rank. You can see why this is not my most popular choice; trains, despite our constant carping about their crap service, are relatively on time compared to busses.

But if I take the train instead of the bus, I arrive at Dorking Mainline Station (no, I didn't make that name up) just four minutes before my connecting train leaves the Dorking Deepdean station. Granted, Deepdean station is not far from the main line station, but I'm not as fit as I used to be and, while younger commuters gladly endure a daily sprint in order to ensure arriving at work on time, it only took one dash out of the station, down the street, around the corner, along the road and up the numerous and steep steps to the Deepdean platform for me to realize this was not something I wanted to make a habit of.

On my next visit, still winded from my first experience, I took a cab. From then on, it became a ritual: I would trot out of the station, hop in the first cab and say, "I have to be at

Deepdean in less than two minutes." More often than not, the driver would mention Deepdean's relative proximity, to which I would reply, "I know, but you can drive there faster than I can run."

At this point the drivers, especially the younger ones, would rise admirably to the challenge, tearing up the road and around the corner as if they were re-enacting scenes from last night's Cops, Camera, Action. After screeching to a halt at the base of the platform, I would toss them a fiver and run up the stairs to the waiting train, sometimes with as much as 20 seconds to spare. It's a little more excitement than I generally want to experience that early in the day, but it got me to work on time and the cabbies couldn't complain about making a fiver for driving a lazy American around the corner. Plus, I had the satisfaction of knowing I beat the system.

Until this morning.

I knew I was in trouble when I saw him reading a newspaper. Still, he was first in line so etiquette demanded I get into his cab.

"I need to be at Deepdean in less than two minutes."

He looked at me over the top of his reading glasses.

"Then you'd be better off walking," he said. "It's just around the corner."

"I know that, but my train is leaving in two minutes and you can drive there faster than I can walk."

Rising to the challenge (albeit not the one I was hoping he'd rise to) he folded his paper, started the car, put it in gear, checked his mirrors, signaled and began driving sedately along the short road. At the corner, he stopped and signaled again before pulling cautiously to the side of the empty street. Ahead of us, the younger commuters had already reached the platform steps and I noted, with growing dismay, that the train was already there.

When we pulled up along the curb, I tried to give him the fiver, but he wasn't having it. He looked at the bill, then fumbled though a wallet, extracted a piece of paper and, with excruciating deliberation, wrote out a receipt. With equal deliberation, he counted out my change and only then accepted my five-pound note.

I leapt from the cab and raced up the stairs, reaching the platform just as the train began pulling away.

Bugger!

All I could do was stand·there, staring at the receding train, empty tracks and the undetermined wait stretching out before me. But then I began to notice other things: birds singing from the nearby shrubbery, buds on the trees, swollen and ready to embrace spring and the morning sun glinting off the dew-covered grass, making it sparkle like emeralds. It was, I noticed, turning into a lovely day and as I stood there—a solitary figure on a deserted railway platform—the sun unveiled the day's beauty and offered the promise of good things to come.

The cabbie, perhaps unknowingly, had done me a favor. Had I made my connection, all of this would have gone unnoticed, and I would be a poorer man for it.

Still, I'm glad I didn't tip him.

Assumptions

We had many adventures during our biannual sojourn to my native land but none were as absurd, nor as exasperating, as those brought about by several basic, and seemingly innocuous, assumptions.

Not being the type of people to leave things to chance, we embarked on our journey with maps, lists of phone numbers, detailed directions and enough paperwork to outfit a midsize bureaucracy. There were a few minor gaps in our data but we (here's that word again) assumed we could patch those holes after we arrived.

And so the adventure began.

We landed in Halifax, toured Nova Scotia, visited Prince Edward Island, drove through New Brunswick and Maine and made it to home territory without once getting lost or even mildly bewildered. Now, maybe it was misplaced confidence in my ability to retain local knowledge after so long an absence, but the few days on home ground often found us maddeningly out of our depth.

Take the simple act of going to my son's apartment.

My son and his fiancée had invited my wife and I out for a Father's Day dinner and had made reservations at a local restaurant. We spent the day visiting friends and then, with naïve optimism, set out for his apartment.

I knew I could find it because he had given detailed directions: "Go one block past the pharmacy, turn right and our building is on the corner." My assumption, as he didn't bother to give me his apartment number, was that his name would be next to his front doorbell. His assumption was that I already knew it.

You have, no doubt, already guessed the outcome: we arrived to find there were no names next to any of the doorbells. Somewhere in one of the sixty-eight apartments my son was wondering where I was and in the car park below I was considering shouting out his name, as if I were in some low-budget re-make of West Side Story, until he poked his head out the window or his neighbors began hurling rotten vegetables. (Incidentally, have you ever wondered about how, in the original West Side Story, Tony manages to wander randomly onto a street in a Puerto Rican neighborhood, shout, "Maria!" and only one woman answers him?)

Anyway, I wasn't too worried because I had his phone number written down so all I needed to do was find a pay phone and call him. This involved the tempting assumption that they hadn't removed all the pay phones since I had lived there, which—as you already know but I did not—they have. Our search for a pay phone took us from one convenience store/gas station/lap dance parlor to another and, when we finally found one, it was vandalized. The second one almost worked (I had to keep shoving the cord back into the handset to get a dial tone) but wouldn't connect me to my son and swallowed all of my change. An increasingly frantic search led me to a working payphone and a need for more change, requiring a stop at a nearby mini-mart.

Armed with Tic-Tacs, a small bag of peanut M&Ms and the resulting change from a five dollar bill I returned to the working phone and called my son. After several frustrating attempts and a lengthy chat with the operator, it came to light that I had written his number down incorrectly.

With no way to contact my son, we returned to his apartment building to see if we could will him to come down by wandering around outside and wishing really hard. When that failed to work we went back to the pay phone and called my other son. All I got was his voice mail. I was going to tell him to call me back but noticed pay phones no longer have their phone numbers on display for the convenience of pimps, crack dealers and absent minded fathers. So I called my friend's house, where we were staying, and left increasingly gibbering messages on his voice mail (for both his cell and home phones) instead.

Every rational avenue for contacting my son had been exhausted, but before we resorted to shouting in the parking lot for him, I had one last, desperate, idea. Knowing the way my mind malfunctions, I was pretty sure I must have transposed some digits when writing down his number. I picked a likely pair, reversed them, dialed this new number and the gods smiled.

He and his fiancée were beginning to worry but when I told him of our plight he was suitably chagrined at not having told us his apartment number. I hung up and headed back to the car, noticing along the way (and I am not making this up) that I had piqued the curiosity of onlookers who couldn't believe someone was actually using a pay phone.

Back at the car I told my wife about the stroke of genius that enabled me to get in touch with my son.

"So what's his apartment number?"

I hesitated.

"Um, I never asked. I just assumed he'd come down to meet us."

Living in Exile

Another business trip. This time to Nottingham—for a week. I'm currently sitting at a sidewalk café across the street from my hotel on something I like to call *Tart Watch*.

Just the word *Nottingham* conjures up images for both Americans and Brits: for the Americans, it brings to mind the exploits of Errol Flynn (or for you younger folks, Kevin Costner) as Robin Hood; for the Brits, it evokes images of gang war, random shootings and particularly nasty muggings (the sort that features a relaxing fortnight in an ICU followed by a varying number of years in a support facility where your daily activities involve drooling, being fascinated by shiny objects and taking your meals through a straw). I am happy to report I have seen neither of these extremes.

True, there are a lot of hints at Robin Hood about: the statue near the castle, *Maid Marian Way*, *Friar Tuck Lane* and a fair number of landmarks named after someone called "Victoria," who must have been Robin's lesser known mistress, or something. The city as a whole reminds me of a guy I used to work with years ago who, if he wasn't on the downward slope of the hill, had at least attained the summit, but still tried to party as if he were 27 and merely ended up looking a bit sad and disheveled despite his new leisure suit. But Nottingham can be forgiven (and rectified, if someone has the ambition to give this place a good once-over with a wire brush and some *Fairy* liquid), especially seeing as how the people here are so friendly and effusive. Every evening at least half a dozen people wander up to me for a spontaneous and surprisingly revealing chat concerning their penchant for missing buses or to tell me about their sick girlfriend who needs an expensive operation and who has also missed her bus, before offering me the opportunity of helping them out by handing over a couple of quid. It's terribly heartwarming, really.

I have made it my habit to sit here every night after work, having a beer and a cigar, to watch the town grow seedy. Early on, there are a lot of people in suits walking purposefully to or from some important meeting, but as the hour grows later, the dress turns—how shall I put this—decidedly casual, with the basic trend favoring piercings, tattoos and a remarkable absence of modesty.

Across from me, I can see a rather large building with a sign designating it as "Dimt." It used to be a popular club but is now unattractively boarded up, lending an air of desperation and urban decay to the surroundings. On the other side of the street is my hotel, The George, recently taken over, but not much improved, by Comfort Inn. I booked the hotel because it was central and seemed a nice place, though the photos and claims about its amenities I found on the Internet tested the line between "exaggeration" and "pure fabrication." It's one of those once-grand hotels that are full of wandering corridors, creaking floors and a vague yet persistent smell of must. My double room is only slightly smaller than your average garden shed and when I expressed my need of an iron and accompanying board to the delightful young lady at the front desk (the one wearing the stud in her lip, not the one with the fetching tattoo on the side of her neck) I was informed they had all been stolen.

Still, it's a congenial enough town and I expect, if I had ample free time, I might find some interesting places to eat and enjoy a convivial pint. As it is, being at work for ten hours a day and having only enough ambition to cross the road after work, I haven't really seen much. Whatever you might have heard, traveling for business is not very glamorous. While I could, if I wanted, have a sumptuous dinner at a posh restaurant every night, I find dining alone too depressing and generally end up visiting a Subway and eating in my room. It's also tiresome being known as the guy who can be relied upon to let you take the extra chairs away from his table because it's obvious he doesn't have any friends.

Even so, I have managed the odd chat that wasn't a prelude to supplication. Just last night I made the acquaintance of Glenn from the NHS who, although surrounded by a baker's dozen of attractive ladies, took the time to provide me with some helpful tips about the locality and directed me to an erstwhile church that had been transformed into a unique and interesting pub. (Thanks, Glenn: that's the second time I've gotten drunk in a church sanctuary, but at least this time it was expected of me.) On another evening, I was joined by a group of lads from Birmingham here for a stag weekend. They had high spirits and blue drinks and moved on as soon as they finished their round. Apparently that's how people drink here—one beer per bar. Clearly there are enough pubs and clubs to accommodate this habit, and the moving on seems never to stop. On my first night here the hooting and hollering went on outside my hotel room window until well after midnight. It gradually eased off around three o'clock only to start up again just as raucously at three-thirty (that must have been the shift change).

How is it that people can drink so late? Don't they have jobs? One would think, if they did have jobs, they would be at home sleeping like a responsible person. And if they don't have jobs, where are they getting the money to drink all night long?

It remains a mystery, and my window, since then, remains closed.

Oh my, here comes a bevy of birds in black dresses with their hemlines where their belts should be. Time to refresh my beverage, light up another cigar and settle in for tonight's episode of *Tart Watch*.

Intermission

We interrupt our regularly scheduled program to bring you this bulletin on the state of British Football.

It's not good.

Now, no one has ever mistaken me for a sports fan, but I do enjoy watching a game now and again. More so since moving to England, primarily due to the fact that British sports tend to be more lively than their American counterparts (we're discounting Cricket here, the sport that makes baseball seem thrilling by comparison). Accordingly, I have grown fond of trips to the local arena with my brother-in-law where we buy a coffee, eat a pork pie and settle in to watch Brighton and Hove Albion run around the pitch for 90 minutes in the rain and cold.

Over the years, it has become a comfortable tradition. But this time it was different: this time it was warm, this time the sun actually appeared, this time there were no pies.

At first, I was in denial. There were four burger coaches on hand; one of them had to sell pies. But it was not to be. I had waited all week for a pie only to be forced into eating a tepid hamburger with a slice of cold cheese on a stale bun. Another piece of England swept away.

I blame the Americans. And, as if to prove me right, we found that the local soccer team now had a cheerleading squad. I say cheerleading squad, but mostly they behaved like a gaggle of girls who were enticed away from a hectic afternoon of hanging around the High Street, dressed up in blue and white outfits and told to wander aimlessly around the perimeter of the field. They were like ants at a picnic—mildly annoying, not supposed to be there, but generally harmless.

But then, at half time, they attempted a routine. This involved waving a few blue and white checkered flags and moving in time to some music. They shouldn't have set their sights so high; any cheerleader who is merely doing something I could do (and quite possibly better) is not worthy of the name.

If I wanted to eat warmed over burgers and watch uninspiring cheerleaders, I'd go back to the States and attend a high school hockey match. What happened to the England I had fallen in love with; is it striving to become a watered down version of America, or has it become accidentally naff?

The thought was so depressing I found myself wishing it would rain, just so it would feel like England again.

But it didn't; instead, the sun came out.

When half time ended, the girls went away and I could concentrate on enjoying the action on the pitch. Although I can't claim to fully understand the rules of soccer, I at least know enough to cheer when they score a goal. I am also savvy enough to recognize the need for a heartfelt groan when someone on our team inadvertently passes the ball to an opposing player. And that's a good thing because, quite frankly, they did this a lot.

They gave the ball away so often I wondered if the coach, during the halftime pep talk, reminded them that the opposing players were the ones in the green jerseys. If he did, they didn't listen. Still, we managed a draw, though the only way either team managed to score a goal was by being allowed to kick it into the opponent's net from about five feet away. That tells you everything you need to know about what sort of game it was.

I was never sure why they allowed them to do this; it was either to avoid having the players go home feeling sad because they didn't get a goal, or the result of (forgive the technical jargon) a really bad penalty.

Speaking of penalties, I had my first experience of seeing one up close, and it saved the day for me. It started when an opposing player dribbled the ball along the pitch in front of us and one of our guys made an enthusiastic, though somewhat unconventional, tackle.

(Aside: "dribbling" refers to running with the ball while kicking it ahead of you and/or to other players, preferably on your own team. I realize the Brits all know this, and very likely most of the Americans know it, as well, but I didn't know it. When I first heard the term, it was in reference to a World War I story concerning a group of boys, destined to have their names chiseled on monuments in their respective village squares, who charged into No Man's Land under heavy machine gun fire during the Battle of Loos while dribbling a football. This conjured up humorous, albeit macabre, images in my mind; although when I found out they were actually kicking a soccer ball and not bouncing an American-style football along the ground, I didn't find it any less bizarre.)

But back to the game. I knew our man had committed a foul, and I knew he would get a yellow card for it. And sure enough, over comes the ref who gives our man a quiet bollocking, holds aloft a yellow card and then, get this, puts it back in his own pocket.

Even through the sound of thousands of fans booing the ref for making such an unfair and outrageous call, I still heard the penny drop. In that instant, gone were my impressions of referees roaming the pitch carrying full decks of yellow cards to hand out to players like points on their drivers licenses. No more would I imagine players saving up the cards to redeem them for a red one after they had acquired enough. It was, in a word, jarring.

So, confused, out of my depth and finding all of my previous assumptions dissipating, I felt, at last, that I truly was in England.

Accidental Tourist

Nottingham again, this time I'm on the 77 Bus en route from my hotel to a client's site and there is a three year old kid sitting behind me singing *The Shut Up Song*. For those of you unfamiliar with this ditty, it goes like this:

Shut up, shut up

Shut up, shut up

Shuuuuut up, shuuuut up

Shut up shut up

This appears to be the only verse, although there is an occasional refrain that sounds something like, "Shut up, shut up, shut shut shut up…" One gets the feeling he has heard that phrase a lot. But the worst part is, it has a tragically catchy tune so I just know it will be with me for the rest of the day.

Still, I prefer this commute to the one I had yesterday.

For this particular commute, I can take the bus, which costs only one pound fifty but takes half an hour, or I can catch a cab, which is more expensive but gets me there ten minutes sooner. I was in a hurry, so I took a cab. I should have walked.

I don't know why I continue to think, "This time will be different," when I have never arrived at my destination from the same direction twice. Nor have I ever successfully conveyed where I want to go without lengthy explanations accompanied by sign language. Don't they make these cabbies do The Knowledge?

At any rate, with misguided optimism, I climbed into the cab and said, "Harvey Road."

"Ardie Road?"

"No, Harvey Road. H - A - R – V…"

"P? Arppie Road?"

"No, 'V' as in 'Very difficult!'"

"'B' in Berry? Arby Road? Are you sure it is in Nottingham? There is no Arby Road in Nottingham."

"It's near the Stadium," I tried.

"What stadium?"

"Harvey Stadium!"

"There is no Arby Stadium."

I dropped my head into my hands and stared at the cab floor. Generally, at this time, a kindly stranger steps in to translate, but there was no one else in the cab, a queue was building up behind us and I knew we were trapped together with our mutual misunderstandings.

The driver pulled away.

"Do not worry," he said, "I will find it."

This failed to fill me with confidence, especially when he reverted to my patented method of trying to find a place by driving aimlessly around and hoping to run into it.

Turns out, there is another stadium in Nottingham, and a Harvey's Haircutting Parlor. I think he drove me past both in the hopes I would get out there. All the while he punched frantically at his SatNav. I was on the verge of telling him to find a 77 bus and follow it when he turned to me in triumph.

"I have found just one Arby Road. Do you think this is it?"

"If it's Harvey Road, it must be."

"Are you sure?"

"If it's Harvey Road, it's got to be the right place."

We set off with renewed, but still misplaced, optimism. I turned my attention to some documents and when I looked up a bit later, expecting to find us nearing our destination, I instead saw a combine harvester and figured we had gone a little bit wrong.

In desperation, I called my office for the client's Post Code. This contained an unfortunate series of G's and B's, so getting the simple code punched into the SatNav required a lay-by, slow, loud and careful word enunciation and much gesticulation. After innumerable attempts, the proper code was entered and we pulled back onto the farm road.

"It is still telling me to go this way," he said. So we did. A hundred yards later the SatNav spoke again.

"It is telling me now to go another way."

We turned off the farm road down a single-track lane. I saw a sign pointing toward Leicester. Sometime later, the roads got wider and I saw signs for Derby, Birmingham and someplace called Loughborough.

By now, we were 45 minutes into a fifteen-minute cab ride and I was too frightened to look at the meter.

Now, please don't think I'm getting all BNP on you; I mean, as an immigrant myself—and one, I am assured, with a distinctive accent—I am the last one you will catch tossing figurative projectiles. I'm just saying, if it were me, and I were in a job that required clear, concise and constant communication with the general public, I might find it advantageous to brush up on my "English as a Second Language" skills.

When we arrived at my actual destination, I looked at the meter.

"You don't expect me to pay that," I said when I stopped choking.

"I asked, 'Are you sure?' You said, 'Yes.'"

There really wasn't any arguing with that. It was, literally, all the money I had. I even needed to dredge through the linings of my coat pockets for spare change to make up the full total. I didn't give him a tip.

It provided a bumpy start to my day, and I'm sure he drove away hoping his next customer wouldn't be so dense when it came to understanding accents.

But next time I find myself faced with an inability to understand or be understood, I think I will heed the advice of the little boy sitting behind me. It would be cheaper.

Getting into the Spirit

Christmas is approaching, so that means the weather is at its most uninspiring, and this morning I awoke to news that a luckless shop worker in Long Island was trampled to death in the Black Friday shopping rush. That's so awful; I mean, it's bad enough to be earning minimum wage at Wal Mart, but to be crushed by the influx of trailer trash shoppers intent on purchasing their $9.99 pink bottle-brush Christmas tree is just too depressing for words.

The news story was broadcast here with barely undisguised glee, as it underscores the greed, selfishness and disregard for human life that, to the rest of the world, is America. It also helps those in the UK to feel morally superior to the US despite the arrest of an MP for exercising freedom of speech and the quashing of taped proof of police brutality during a trial in order to obtain a favorable verdict (favorable to the police, at any rate).

All this was revealed during a five minute news break while I was attempting to enjoy my breakfast. Now you see why I try to avoid the news over here; nothing good really comes out of listening to it.

The local news isn't much better. Our resident shopping mall—the providers of our holiday consumer joy—have banned a popular, local waif from selling magazines (her only source of income) from the beneath the shelter of the large awning that graces the main entrance. She now has to stand in the rain, just beyond the safety of the overhang. When asked for comment, the spokesperson for the mall merely affirmed that the area under the awning was private property. Now, that is unquestionably the letter of the law but, considering the season, these people living off of our shopping addictions come across as real parsimonious pricks.

But it's not all doom and gloom. The town center lights this year are really pretty, and I managed to start off the official holiday season with a memorable Thanksgiving feast, even if it wasn't turkey.

In an attempt to avoid the yearly heartbreak of trying—and failing—to recreate a traditional Thanksgiving dinner in the UK, my wife decided to take us out to dinner instead. We went to our town's poshest restaurant where, instead of enjoying a turkey with all of the trimmings, I had to content myself with spending the average annual wage of a Bangladeshi teenager working in the Nike factory on a single meal.

It was fantastic. I'm here to tell you that food, when it is not being served by teenagers wearing hairnets and nametags, is really quite a treat. The only drawback was that, as it was a swanky joint, the cuisine was of the Nuevo variety, meaning large plates adorned with small portions of artfully arranged food. That, in itself, wasn't bad, as I finished the meal feeling satisfied but not stuffed. But I made the mistake of effusing about the meal to my wife, prompting her to start serving meals consisting of half a fish-stick criss-crossed with three potato wedges and surrounded by seven peas. It's artistically satisfying, if nothing else, especially with the elegant swish of ketchup across the top of the plate.

Good thing there's an Indian take-out just across the street.

Singing in the Rain

Despite our valiant efforts to catch up to the 19th century—we now have actual heaters in the sitting room and our bedroom—I can still count on the frigid air in the unheated hallway and bathroom to snap me awake as I stumble around in the dark every morning. And these past days, with the temps dipping down into previously uncharted depths, it has snapped me awake quite sharply.

This morning, as I prepared for the day, I noticed it was not nearly as cold, so I knew there had been a change in the weather. And I was right; it's raining.

But this isn't light, misty, well-mannered English rain; this is angry, lashing, why-didn't-I-move-to-Majorca-when-I-had-the-chance rain. So I did what I normally do when the weather is bad: I walked from my heated kitchen into my attached, heated garage, got into my heated car, pressed the garage door opener, drove to work and parked in the underground lot and took a heated elevator to my heated office.

Sorry, that was me daydreaming about America. Here in the real world, I walk out into the storm, wait for a bus, sit on the bus with 57 other similarly drenched commuters and, having marginally dried off, receive a fresh coating of rain as I walk to my office so I can arrive looking as if someone just sprayed me with a fire hose.

Before all you Americans start thinking, "What sort of bollocks is this?" (or whatever you think in America these days) and you Brits turn to a more interesting page with a dismissive, "Yeah, it's raining, so what?" allow me to explain how this can make life just a bit more interesting, informative and potentially convenient.

First of all, I rarely experienced rain in the US, at least not on such intimate terms (precipitation participation, perhaps?) and on those rare occasions when I did find myself in a deluge, I was not as prepared for it as I am this morning. Here I have weather gear I didn't even know existed, so when I stepped into the storm, I was fully ensconced in my survival apparel, gloved, hooded, Velcroed at every seam and carrying a briefcase in one hand and a pile of Christmas cards (destination US) in the other.

It's interesting to be in a gale and hear the wind whistling around your hood and feel the rain drumming on your back but still remain slightly detached from it, as if you're in a bathysphere exploring the Marinas Trench and knowing only in an academic sense that, just beyond the confines of your personal space, it is very, very wet.

What I'm finding informative is the bus ride.

I know it's hard to believe, but there's a deep sense of satisfaction gained from braving the blizzards of New York. When you arrive at work, you look around at the others who made the treacherous trek and exchange silent, solemn nods; acknowledgments of the bond you share with your fellow adventurers. Your absent colleagues? Well, they're all pussies, aren't they?

But in England, bereft of snow (no, I mean *real* snow; spend a winter in Saratoga County, then come talk to me), we have to content ourselves with being brave in the face of rain.

And so it is this morning, with the bus carrying only half of its usual passengers: those who aren't here—the fair-weather greens who retreat to their cars at the first sign of inconvenience and the students with the luxury of just staying home when it suits them (I may be making a rash judgment here but, as I look around me, I see more briefcases than book bags)—serve as absent affirmations of our fortitude and resilience.

Or maybe they're all like me and simply have no other way of getting to work.

And lastly, I think I might have found a way of making being drenched in the morning work for me. Remember the cards I was carrying, the end result of countless hours of work by my wife—who hand-made the cards, filled them out and addressed the envelopes—and endless minutes of grumbling and procrastination by me—who had to sign them? Well, they don't react agreeably to water.

In my defense, I didn't believe it was raining as hard as it was before I ventured outside, and once I did, what was I do to? I couldn't penetrate my survival gear while holding cards and a briefcase and wearing ungainly gloves, and even if I could, it wouldn't have been a wise thing to do. So I tucked the cards under my arm and sheltered them as best I could on the slog to the mailbox.

As you might imagine, it did little good. By the time I got there, the cards were soaked and decorated with fetching little monochrome watercolor paintings that used to be addresses.

And wouldn't you know it, this was the year I sent cards to simply everybody back in the States—my friends, relatives, casual acquaintances and, yes, even you—but I doubt the cards will get there now. Darn that rain!

So, if you're in America, and you don't get a Christmas card from me this year, don't think it was because you were left off the list, blame the rain.

Or the fact that I don't have a heated garage.

The Annual Office Party

Office Christmas (er, Holiday) Party last night. Five o'clock alarm this morning. Bus to work right now. Not a good combination. I have felt worse in my day, and handled it better, but I was younger then, and better equipped to take such things in stride. When you're hung over every morning, it becomes part of your day, but once you embrace the advantages of sobriety—such as not waking up in the flower bed with a stray dog licking your face and a tattered cocktail napkin from Pinkie's Disco and Dance Emporium stapled to your lapel with, "Call me!" scrawled across it in eye-liner—you come to expect a higher degree of lucidity during the morning hours, or at least to remember where you left your shoes.

So, yeah, I got a bit tipsy last night, because nothing beats getting embarrassingly drunk with people you avoid social contact with throughout the remainder of the year. I don't know how many free books I promised last night, but if everyone holds me to it, it will need to be a best seller in order for me to break even.

Other than that, it was your typical office party—much maligned beforehand but more fun than you thought it would be once it got going; sort of like bowling. Even the awards ceremony (Biggest Bullshitter, Most Dedicated Hoarder, things like that; really, you could die laughing) turned out to be a surprisingly good time, although I suspect the four pints of lager and half a bottle of wine had something to do with that. Nothing turns a bad idea into a good idea quicker than alcohol—I'm sure the decision to stick a fireworks rocket up his butt and have his buddy set a match to it (I actually saw this on YouTube) was fueled by at least a few cans of lager. Or at least one hopes so.

But getting back to my misery: this morning, of all days, I encountered, for the first time since moving here, sidewalks (excuse me, pavements) covered in ice. Given my fragile condition and the fact that several ice-free years have resulted in a remarkable decrease in my ice navigating skills, the short walk to the bus stop was more interesting than I would have preferred.

It has been brought to my attention that I am becoming something of a weather weenie, but I can't refute it; living in southern England has made me soft. In New York, the weather was famously awful. During one particularly memorable winter, I became so fed up with the snow I seriously considered moving. In my search for a new locale, I enlisted the aid of a *Good Places to Live* website and discovered, without surprise, that the Albany region was displayed very near the bottom of the list. The main reason was the climate, which it termed as "harsh." (Other reasons had to do with mind-numbing boredom and in-breeding.) Basically, it advised you not to move there.

In the end, it wasn't the weather that caused me to leave the States (though come to think of it, maybe that's why I drank so much when I lived there), but the upgrade in the climate has proven to be an unexpectedly pleasant peripheral benefit.

Consider this: I haven't had to shovel my roof since 2001, and I don't need to take the distributor cap out of my car and put it in the oven to warm it up so the car will start (no, really, it got that cold where I used to live). My pipes have never frozen here, I don't have to wear heavy boots and I don't even own a snow shovel.

I don't know what any of that has to be with being hung over; I guess my mind isn't firing on all cylinders this morning. At any rate, the bus is nearly at my office so I need to pack up my mobile desk and face the day.

I just hope my workmates will have the good grace to claim they don't remember me promising all those free books

Man Shopping

This may surprise you but, as the 20th of December dawned, I had not yet finished my Christmas shopping. Although I had managed, several times, to carve out sufficient blocks of time when I was home and my wife was not, which would have allow me a leisurely afternoon of purchasing and wrapping, circumstances conspired to keep my "to buy" list long and my wife's gift pile alarmingly smaller than mine.

Today was my final chance. My wife was off to London for a day at the theater with friends to see Brother Cadfael playing Malvolio in *Twelfth Night*, leaving me to my long overdue tasks. She was to leave at ten-thirty. To get a jump on the day, I left at nine o'clock to go shopping. I was back by ten. This was only possible because I engage in something I like to call, "Man Shopping." Had I engaged in "Woman Shopping," I wouldn't have finished before tea time.

Woman shopping involves a lot of touching. "Oooh, feel this," is an expression often heard in this style of shopping. Don't get me wrong, I like shopping with my wife but, to my way of thinking, it isn't really shopping; it's just wandering around the stores feeling things. Often, my wife doesn't even buy anything, so how can you call it shopping if you come home with nothing? And the thing I really hate about woman shopping is hearing myself saying things like, "That's a lovely blouse; if you match it with that skirt over there it would look quite smart." That's when I start wondering if there's too much estrogen in my diet and thinking I should go off on my own to look at power tools.

Conversely, man shopping is a mission; you have an objective, you achieve it, you're done. Simple as that.

I knew exactly what I wanted because, as a veteran of matrimony, I know enough to not let Christmas sneak up on me. Throughout the year, if I see something I think my wife might want for Christmas, I make note of it. You newlywed guys listen up, this may save your marriage: sometimes when you are out on a touch and feel excursion with your wife, she might hint that some item would make a nice Christmas gift for her. She might, for instance, say, "See that item over there, on the second shelf, the blue one? I want that for Christmas." This is a clear hint. So do what I do. Make a note of it. Then forget where you left the note and hope your wife reminds you again.

So, list in hand, I walked into town. In the first shop, I went straight to the counter and told the clerkess, "See that..." (In the interest of preserving my wife's pleasant surprise on Christmas morning, I obviously can't say what sort of shop I was in or what I was buying, so you ladies can just insert your fantasy gift here: Tiffany Jewelry, Chanel No 5, that item in Ann Summers you just can't summon up the nerve to buy for yourself.) "...I want that." She looked at me, puzzled for a moment, before it dawned on her that even though I hadn't looked at every item in the store before going back to the one I had looked at first, I was, indeed, shopping. She fetched it; I bought it. Objective achieved.

Another tactic I like to use is to walk into a shop (this works best in shops that sell lady type things) and just stand there with a baffled and slightly panicked look on my face. Within seconds a store clerk will come up to me and ask if she can help, and I say, "Yes, I need a..." (Again, for the sake of secrecy: new ironing board cover, really nice set of pots, gift certificate for a full-color tattoo.) She gets, I buy. Next stop.

I even had time to make an impulse buy while I was out. Returning through the market square, I noticed a new kiosk selling beer, so I vectored over and a six-pack of holiday ales jumped into my hand (oddly, fourteen quid jumped out of my wallet at the same time).

My wife was only mildly surprised to see me back so soon. I hid her gifts until she left and then wrapped them. They are now under the tree and our respective gift piles are more or less equal (actually, I think she's winning at this point) and I suddenly find myself without adult supervision and the bulk of the day before me.

I think I hear a bottle of ale calling from the other room. It's saying I should take it out on the balcony with a nice cigar and enjoy the uncharacteristically mild weather.

Who am I to argue?

Built to Last

For the past six months or so, our toilet hasn't stopped running. We did all the right things—jiggled the flush handle, took the top off the cistern and fiddled with the ballcock (hey now, none of that; keep your mind on the story) and stared quizzically into the rust-stained depths. Nothing worked. We probably could have gone on like this for another six months but lately the trickle developed ambitions toward becoming a waterfall and the prospect of having to trot down to the local mall to use their facilities didn't appeal to us, so we did what we always do when we run out of options: we called the landlord.

To digress a bit, I don't like calling the landlord. Now, it may simply have been luck that allowed me to enjoy a succession of responsive and responsible landlords before I moved to Britain (except for that guy who ran the cocaine business out of his workshop and then torched it to suppress evidence just before the T-men—armed with dogs, crime-scene tape and automatic weapons—swooped in at dawn and gave us 24 hours to vacate the apartments we had been renting from him) but my landlord here is sort of like the government: a faceless and uncaring bureaucracy that, on a good day, simply ignores you. This bureaucracy masquerading as a landlord has morphed and grown and eaten smaller, less fortunate landlords over the years and is currently headquartered in Jersey (the fetching, Channel Island tax-dodge, not the Mafia-infested, chemical waste dump) where, like an aging mob-boss, it lounges in luxury, shielded from inconvenient codicils in the tenancy agreements by a larceny of lawyers (that is the collective noun for lawyers, isn't it?) and generally makes me wish I had the cocaine-dealer back.

This, recall, is a multinational, billion pound conglomerate that owns a gazillion buildings, so you might expect to reach a byzantine, recorded call system that wastes your time for half an hour then cuts you off without offering any help, or at least a call center in Bangladesh, which will do the same but less efficiently. That would be an improvement; as it is, when I ring up their Emergency Repair Service Hot Line, I'm connected to Cindy (sorry, she prefers Cynthia) who apparently spends a great deal of her day hanging around the water cooler being chatted up by the guys in Finance because the only way I can get her on the phone is by calling every half hour or so for a day and a half, and then, after being corrected on the pronunciation of her name, all I get for my trouble is her promise to call the contractor. Now, sometimes she does and sometimes she doesn't but, whatever the outcome, the contractor has a habit of not calling me, preferring to show up unannounced at an empty flat, which then precipitates accusatory calls wanting to know why we're out earning a living instead of sitting at home watching *Cash in the Attic* on the off-chance a contractor might happen by.

But it didn't seem as if the toilet was going to heal itself, so we drew straws to see who would have to call Cynthia. I lost.

The negotiations took less than a week, and on the appointed day, the contractor showed up bright and early.

Good thing.

It was supposed to be a ten-minute job but when the contractor assessed the toilet with an awed, "My God! I haven't seen one of these in thirty years!" I think we both understood we were in for a long day.

The problem turned out to be a simple washer, but the requisite part was last manufactured when The Beatles were still an unknown pub band and, after two hours of heroic jerry-rigging, the toilet still wouldn't shut off. I was, the contractor informed me, in possession of an Imperial Toilet, or at least the kind that uses the imperial measuring system. Britain uses metric, and has for some time, so there was no way he could get a part to fit the flushing mechanism without a trip to the British Museum. What he would have to do—for want of an imperial washer—was replace the entire thing.

This, in itself, wasn't a problem; the problem became apparent only after we discovered that, when my flat was constructed at the close of the Boer War, the builders cemented the toilet into the floor, apparently unable to conceive of the possibility that it might someday wear out (which, indeed, it had not) or that the metric system might breach the Channel (which, unfortunately, it had).

And so, armed only with a miniature jackhammer, safety goggles and a complete disregard for anyone within a half-mile radius who might work the night shift, the contractor did battle with the toilet, emerging forty-five minutes later with my old toilet in remarkably good condition and my bathroom looking like someone had dropped a wrecking ball onto the floor and then bumped it up against the walls for good measure.

I give him credit, he did a remarkable job of covering up the damage, and he promised to come back next week to fix the walls, but the real trick came in seating the new toilet. While the original builders at least had the option of cementing the toilet in place, they left any future handymen nothing to go on but lateral thinking. I left him to it and checked in an hour later to find he had glued it to the floor with an industrial strength bonding gel. Fair enough; it's not like he had a choice, but you know that in three years time, when this toilet breaks and the EU has foist some other dodgy measurement system off on us and the contractor can't get parts for it, he's going to be back in there with the jackhammer.

It's sad to have to resign oneself to such a scenario, but I cannot think of anything I have purchased since around 1967 that was built with such quality, ruggedness and anticipated longevity as my erstwhile Imperial Toilet.

You Say Skaun, I Say Skown

One of the many unexpected perks I discovered after my arrival in Britain was the ready availability of scones. There is nothing like a warm, fresh scone with a nice cup of tea and I had my favorite locations for obtaining them and enjoying a relaxing half hour or so in their company. To the nation's detriment, this—like derby hats and bucket-and-spade holidays—is becoming a thing of the past.

There used to be two nice tea shops in my little town. Now there is just one, and it is no longer nice. We can get a Grande Moca-chinno Latte in any random establishment, but we can only use it to wash down a Double Chocoholic Muffin or a croissant.

There are, naturally, places where scones are served but, more and more, they seem to be of the raisin or cheese varieties. What is with that? Why take a perfectly good scone and dress it up with fruit or dairy products? That's what strawberry jam and clotted cream are for!

Even my old standby, The National Trust, has fallen victim to scone perversions. Time was, a trip to a National Trust property was not complete without a visit to the café for a buttered scone and a cup of tea. The scones they served were generous and warm and practically melted in your mouth. So good were they, that I was going to devote a whole chapter to them in a book I was planning on writing one of these days called, "Scones I have Known."

Obviously, I was counting on an American audience to buy this book, where the rhyme would make sense. Over here, they often pronounce "scone" to rhyme with "lawn," so there would have been a few marketing difficulties to overcome. But despite this apparent deal-breaker, I doggedly continued my research, savoring scones in Cumbria, Wales, Scotland, Yorkshire and even Surrey. Occasionally I would chance upon some raisin or cheese infused concoction masquerading as a scone, but I wasn't fooled, and there were always plenty of real scones nearby.

Then, rather swiftly, the ratio of scones to fruit and cheese pastries shifted until I found myself, this past weekend, actually making scones, just so I could have one without raisins in it. (I apologize for undertaking such as task without coming away with a raft of amusing anecdotes concerning my kitchen misadventures, but it appears I have been here long enough to master British cooking implements: I made scones. They were good. End of story. Did you laugh?)

What can I say; maybe next time I'll take on something more challenging—like hunting down a real scone in the wild. Baking is all well and good, but going out to a tea shop and sitting down to a scone you don't have to wash up after has a higher satisfaction to drudgery ratio. Plus I can't feature my own scones in the book; how would that look?

Right now, my hopes are pinned on the posh afternoon tea we're soon to attend. Through a series of circumstances too complex to go into (except to say it involved me dressing up as a cartoon bear) we won a raffle prize, which was afternoon tea at the Ghyll Manor Hotel. The name means just as much to me as it does to you but I am assured this is a swanky joint and that they put on a splendid tea. It would really be a disappointment if we got there and I had to embarrass my wife by picking the raisins out of my scone as a roomful of well-heeled octogenarians looked on and quietly tsk tsked behind my back

I suppose I could rename my book, "Scone With the Wind" and market it to a UK audience. In it, I could reminisce about the defunct Sussex Tea Shoppe and That Other Place before it went downhill. I could recapture the halcyon days of the National Trust Café, when they served those wonderful, non-raisin, no-cheese scones in a Britain where it was always sunny, men wore derby hats and families spent their weekends at the seaside.

On second thought, that might sell better in America; the British know better.

The Perfect Block

If they include "Aisle Blocking" in the 2012 Olympics, Britain can rest easy: they are assured of the Gold.

For those of you not familiar with this activity, "Aisle Blocking" is the popular sport of blocking supermarket aisles in creative ways using only your body and a shopping trolley. It's something the British seem to have a special talent for, and I encounter many enthusiastic amateurs each time I visit Waitrose.

In the organized sport, there are several divisions:

- Solo Division: this is the more difficult division, but it enjoys a dedicated following. It involves strategic positioning and precise calculations of the cart/body mass ratio
- Tandem Division: this involves a friend with a cart and a long conversation
- Children's Division: This involves one or more child (defined by the ABC—Aisle Blocking Commission— as under the age of 12). NOTE: The children must be on their own; if they are with a parent they are considered "Assets" (see Rules below)

Rules:

- Basically, you block the aisle. (It's the simple sports that are the most elegant, don't you think?)
- The blocking must be accomplished using only your body and your cart to be worth any points. Using a child as an Asset automatically relegates your Block to the Tandem Division.
- Use of NLAs (Non-Living Assets, such as support columns, stock carts or store employees) is not allowed; these are classified as Obstacles.

After first noticing this phenomenon and making an initial study of it, I moved on to other things, but I never forgot about it (after all, I still have to shop at least once a week). Occasionally, I would notice an impressive block but, to be blunt, I was getting a bit bored with the lackluster performances I was seeing lately. It's as if people stopped caring.

But last night, while doing our weekly shop, I encountered the most heartwarming sight:

As we rounded the corner of one aisle and did a sort of U-bend to make our way to the other section of the store, we came upon a young woman in the Solo Division who was blocking people, not just from moving up and down the aisle, but from accessing an entire section of the store, using only her slender self and a wire shopping basket that contained nothing but a liter of orange juice.

It was poetry immobile.

She had placed the basket on the floor, perfectly positioned to make it impossible to pass by on one side, while she stood in the wider gap, talking on her mobile phone. (There was discussion within the ABC about whether or not the phone should be considered an Asset but they ruled that people can be just as vapid and clueless with or without a phone.)

It was a rare privilege to see someone at the peak of their game, displaying their skills with such casual grace. She was definitely Olympic material and I considered it an honor to be in her presence. So awestruck was I that I would have happily stood there for ten minutes or so admiring this genius at work (which was apparently the length of time she was planning to spend yakking on her phone) but my enthusiasm got the better of me and I involuntarily exclaimed, "Oh my God! That's brilliant!" (No, I am not making that up; I really do spend our shopping trips commenting on people's blocking maneuvers. You have no idea what my wife has to put up with.)

I didn't mean to put her off her game, but disappointingly, she glanced at me with a look of mild annoyance and grudgingly stepped aside. Even so, the experience was thrilling, and I couldn't help commenting on it as we walked past her toward the Coffee, Tea and Biscuits aisle.

"That was inspiring! She's a shoo-in for a silver, at least!"

My wife studied the biscuit selection, attempting to ignore me. "You're going to get into trouble someday, you know."

My only regret was that I didn't have anything on me for her to autograph. I suppose I could have asked her to sign our shopping list, but we were only half done and my wife wouldn't give it up. Still, when I see her on the podium at the Olympic Games, I'll be able to say I saw her in action.

Hobbies

If you were looking to commit a crime in West Sussex, you missed your golden opportunity; this past weekend, every policeperson in southern England was busy guarding the world's elite…in my very town! (Actually, it was in Lower Beeding, a tiny village just below Horsham but, ironically, well above Upper Beeding.)

There were so many squad cars here I originally thought they were holding a police convention. I was therefore surprised to see a few policepersons keeping the crowds in line at the Brighton football match on Saturday afternoon. They must have borrowed them from Yorkshire, or else they were "Hobby Bobbies."

Yes, Hobby Bobbies: in Britain, if you have a hankerin' to be a police officer, you can actually volunteer to take on the role, with no pay. They are, I am told, well trained and come with nearly all the powers of an actual police officer, but they do so on their personal time just for the fun of it. In the US, if you want to experience the thrill of being a cop (i.e. being legally allowed to threaten people with a gun) you have to get a part-time job as a security guard.

I thought playing at being a policeman an odd thing for grownups to be doing in their spare time until it occurred to me that, where I lived for the first 36 years of my life, if your house was burning down, the guys coming to put it out weren't professional firemen, but your milkman, the bank manager, your daughter's gymnastics instructor, the kids who works at the dairy farm down the road and the guy who sits outside the drug store shouting at pigeons and dinking from a bottle wrapped in a brown paper bag. Likewise, if you were in a serious car accident, or had a heart attack, the Emergency Medical Technicians who came to your rescue might be your mailman, the produce manager at the Grand Union or the director of the local funeral home (this is the absolute truth; he was a good EMT, but I still think it was a conflict of interest).

It wasn't until I moved to a more populated area that I encountered the concept of paid, professional fire fighters and ambulance crews. And initially, that idea seemed odd. What did all those people do in their spare time if not hang around the firehouse cleaning their equipment and drinking beer? Our volunteer organizations weren't just about keeping people's houses from burning down; they were more of a social club.

The downside to this, as one might guess, is that people who volunteer to be firemen tend to be the type of people who like to fight fires and, occasionally, when things are a little slow, they might, shall we say, encourage some activity. We had a spate of particularly suspicious fires one summer and the pair of brothers who set them were members of the local fire company. They got caught when the police became suspicious because they were high-fiving each other at one of the fires. Idiots.

In England, in addition to spending your spare time as an unpaid cop, you can join the St. John's Ambulance organization and spend your spare time as an unpaid EMT. The downside to that is, because all of the local authorities in Britain have their own paid emergency services, volunteer ambulance crews are only allowed to provide first aid until the real ambulance crew shows up. Not quite as glamorous as it is for the guy who clerks part-time at the drug store but gets to use the Jaws-of-Life to pry local drunks out of their wrecked vehicles on Saturday nights.

Perhaps the coolest volunteer job you can get here is on a lifeboat rescue crew. These hardy souls brave storms, wind, waves and worrisome wives to row out and save over-optimistic boaters. So if you ever find yourself swamped by a sudden squall off the coast of Cumbria and clinging for life to a bit of wood in twenty-foot swells, know that the people rowing out to rescue you are, more likely than not, just a bunch of enthusiastic amateurs.

Still, I suppose it could be worse; at least you'd know they were doing it because they enjoyed it, not because the dole money ran out and, when they schlepped down to the Job Centre, "Rowboat Rescue Crew" sounded marginally more appealing than "Tesco Shelf Stocker" because it offered the possibility of down time. And, of course, you could be fairly certain it wasn't one of them who sank your boat.

Silver Linings, Dark Clouds

The week started off innocuously enough, but here it is Thursday and I'm out over £1,000, we have no heat in the sitting room and we can't watch the TV.

Allow me to elucidate:

When I got home last Friday, I put my bus pass (recently renewed at no small cost) down somewhere and set about enjoying a weekend snug in my warm sitting room watching CSI on the telly with my wife. The first cracks appeared on Sunday afternoon when we noticed it was getting a bit chilly. A quick check of the heater confirmed it was broken.

In order to appreciate the significance of this, you have to know the history of our heaters. When we first moved in, the original storage heaters were still operating as they had been since VE Day. There was one in the hallway and one in the sitting room; we turned them on in the autumn and had heat (whether we wanted it or not) in the sitting room and hallway, and none (whether we needed it or not) in the bedrooms and bathroom until spring arrived and we felt it safe to turn them off. This is how you have to play it with storage heaters; you can't just get up on a frosty October morning, flick a switch and expect instant heat. You have to plan your heating needs at least a fortnight in advance. (Conversely, if you turn them off on May Day, they'll still be warm at Whitsun.) The heat in my US apartment operated on the "Shock and Awe" method—there in spades when you needed it—but here, it's more like sending a runner to fetch the infantry and hoping they arrive before the war is over.

Then one day, some years ago, the heater in the hallway went to that great landfill in the sky (or, more likely, just outside of Basingstoke). The sad thing was, we had no idea when it expired; it went cold in January but, for all we knew, it might have packed up on Pearl Harbor Day, only to continue mindlessly spewing heat from its dead appliance body like a headless chicken flopping about in a barnyard. After untold years of loyal service, its death throes went unnoticed and it was unceremoniously turned off without the dignity of a proper expiry date. We shed a tear, took a deep breath and called the landlord.

That was on Tuesday. I managed to get through to Cynthia before Friday and, as usual, she promised to call the contractor.

A few weeks later, after we had resigned ourselves to a frigid hallway and began using the heater as a small table, a man named Terry called to tell me he had been asked to replace my heaters. Terry was a man who knew how to get things done.

"I understand your heaters are broken," he said.

"Well, actually, only one is broken. But since you are coming over, could you replace both of them."

"I can only replace a heater if it's broken," he said, enunciating each word. "So which heater is broken?"

I thought for a second, attempting to comprehend.

"Oh, they both are."

"Good. We'll replace both of them, then."

He went silent while he wrote something on a note pad.

"Okay," he said. "So which is the broken one?"

Was this a test? I thought it over and decided to stay in character.

"They're both broken," I said.

Terry sighed.

A few days later, Terry and his apprentice came over and, with much banging and drilling and the dragging of heavy pieces of materials around, managed to make us believe they were doing major work. But when they left, we discovered all they had done was remove the old heaters and affix two cheap, auxiliary electric heaters—the kind you might stick under your desk in a cold office—on the walls in their place. These, at least, gave instant heat. They also turned the walls black. So we unscrewed them from their fittings, put them on the floor and moved bookcases to cover the black spots. And so life went on.

A year later they stopped working. We couldn't see going through all that aggravation again just for the opportunity of darkening the walls some more, so we went to the local Homebase and bought new ones ourselves. And now, after only a year, the one in the sitting room had stopped working. Again.

We wrapped up in jumpers and blankets, said a prayer to the heater gods and proposed to call the Landlord on Monday barring divine intervention.

Monday arrived, the heater was still broken and I couldn't find my bus pass. I ended up having to buy a weekly ticket for twenty quid.

At work, I spent much of the day tracking down my good friend Cynthia. As before she assured me she would tell someone about my plight and, a few hours later, the contractor called. (I don't know why she just doesn't give me the contractor's number, except that would put her out of a job.)

I explained the situation, complete with blackened walls and accounts of the unreliability of the product.

"We can't replace it, then," he said.

"Why not? We're in an apartment with no heat. We're supposed to have heat; it's in the rental agreement."

"It's not our heater. We can't replace it."

"But your heaters broke; we replaced them ourselves."

"That's why we can't replace it; it's not one we installed."

He wasn't enunciating his words so, unlike Terry, I didn't think he was attempting to lead me to the correct answer. Before resigning myself to buying another heater, I gave it one last try:

"Are you telling me," I said, "that because we did you a favor, you are now penalizing us and, for the rest of eternity, you will never install another heater in this flat?"

"Okay," he sighed. "Leave it in the hallway and I'll see what I can do."

When I got home, we still couldn't find my bus pass but we had thin hopes of getting some heat soon. We spent another night cocooned in quilts and I put the broken heater outside the door when I left for work the next morning, expecting it to be gone and a new, working one, in its place when I returned.

Upon my arrival, I found he had, indeed, removed the broken heater, but had left no replacement, no explanation and no idea what we should do about it.

On Wednesday I still couldn't find my bus pass, but with my weekly pass due to expire in a few days I fast-forwarded through the "disbelief, bargaining and anger" stages of my lost bus pass grief and arrived at "acceptance" around ten o'clock in the morning so I could order a new one at lunchtime. The only good thing to come out of the debacle was that I discovered my bus company now offered a yearly pass, which was more of a bargain than the quarterly tickets I had been buying. So I made what I could out of that glint of sunshine and loaded up my credit card with a year's worth of bus rides.

Back at home, still no heater, still no word from the contractor or Cynthia, and the television stopped working. I think it froze to death.

We were a bit shocked by this because it was only seven years old and we both know for a fact that, when we were young, television sets lasted for decades, but these days all you get is cheap junk and...(come on, you know the words, sing along with me). So we proposed to buy a new TV set.

I then told my wife that I had purchased a new bus pass and how much it cost. She winced (she's part Scottish, she can't help it) but agreed that the yearly pass was a better deal. I also told her that, according to Sod's Law, my lost bus pass would now turn up.

"How could it?" she said. "We've looked everywhere."

"We'll probably find it when we move the old TV."

"How could it possibly be under the telly?"

"I don't know. It could be under anything."

To prove my point, I lifted a box of tissues. There was my bus pass.

We tried not to think about it. We ate a silent dinner, then walked to Curry's to further burden my credit card.

Back at the flat, our spirits buoyed somewhat by our consumerism fix, we hooked up our new, fully digital, HD-ready telly and initiated the boot-up sequence. It managed to automatically pick up every channel except the ones we routinely watch. So we can now see shows we don't want to watch in a picture so crystal clear it makes you want to weep, but we can't get any of the programs we really like.

My wife is inconsolable. And we still have no heat in the sitting room.

But at least with my brand new yearly bus pass, my rediscovered quarterly bus pass and a weekly bus pass, I am practically assured of getting a seat on the bus tomorrow morning.

Wishing to Know

My mother died when I was a young man. That was many years ago, and now that I have attained an age where I can ruminate on things past, I find there are many questions I wish I had been able to ask my mother when she was alive.

Such as: where did you get the idea that Campbell's Tomato soup was a viable substitute for spaghetti sauce? I grew up believing that pasta was supposed to be pink and taste like the inside of a tin can. And what was with the chopped up Spam? Who told you we liked Spam; certainly not us.

And butter; you made me believe that butter was as expensive as gold and that was why we had to put up with the crappy, cheap margarine you always bought. It wasn't until I was much older that I realized butter was easily within my budget, but by then I was being forced—by a succession of well-meaning girlfriends—to use butter substitutes for health reasons. You consigned me to a life without butter? Why?

And if you were really concerned about saving money, why didn't you buy a sack of natural rice instead of buying expensive boxes of Minute Rice? How could you have been pressed for time when you didn't even have a job? If you could have seen your way toward investing more than 10 minutes of your busy day toward food preparation, you could have made real rice and served up something that didn't taste quite so much like cardboard. Then the money you saved could have been used toward buying whole milk instead of that powdered stuff you foisted off on us. You were salutatorian of your graduating class, for chrissake; surely you could have done the math.

What was that powdered milk all about, anyway? Who thought that was a good idea? How come I never saw dad drinking powdered beer?

And where did you get the haggis? A few years ago, after moving to England, I tried haggis and discovered two surprising things: a) I liked it, and b) I had eaten it before. You fed me haggis! I realize dad's family was from England, but we were in America; did the relatives back in Lancashire keep them supplied with Scottish novelty foods? Was that how you were able to serve it to me? And, if this is the case, why wasn't I

113

taken into foster care? Were there no child protection agencies operating at the time?

All that being said, you made Christmas cookies like no one else, and on Easter, you made that wonderful Easter Egg Cake.

It was filled with a concoction of shredded coconut, sugar, corn syrup and powdered raspberry Jell-o, covered in a thick layer of dark chocolate and decorated with green icing. It was shockingly sweet and bad for you in about ten different ways; everything an Easter treat should be. Over the years I have tried to recreate this legendary confection but each effort has fallen flat.

Still, after all these years, when the season of Lent draws to an end, my memory is tugged back to a time when I would watch you shape the crimson, coconut egg and lovingly slather it with melted chocolate. What I wouldn't give for just one more taste of that egg, or the chance to watch as you carefully crafted it while I stood by, anticipating the first tart taste.

If I had the chance to talk to you again, for just five minutes, that's all I would want to know: how on earth did you make that heavenly cake?

That, and where did you get the haggis?

Sconed

Remember that cream tea I won for my wife by dressing up in a bear costume? The one I was looking forward to so I could get a real scone and not something dressed up in cheese and or infused with raisins? Well, this past weekend, we went to Ghyll Manor and cashed in our voucher.

The story behind this is just long enough to maintain your interest, but not long enough to bore you to tears, and, most importantly, it will allow me to bulk up the word count a bit: the event we attended was a Children In Need fund raising gala. This involved a bit of barn dancing, food, and the purchase of many raffle tickets. Due to the fact that I never win anything, I am free to buy raffle tickets without having to worry about what the prize is; to me, it's a straight donation.

As you know, they pulled my ticket. But not only that, they pulled it first, and I had my pick of the prizes. Initially, I reached for a bottle of whiskey (really, what would you expect?) but then a survival instinct kicked in (that same one that forces you to remember your anniversary every year about a week before it rolls around) and I recalled my wife pointing out the "cream tea at a posh hotel" prize and remarking that it was a really, really good one. So I took that, instead.

The part that involves me inside of a bear suit came about because I made the mistake of milling around looking as if I had nothing to do, which, in truth, I did not. The organizer spotted me and asked, with seeming innocence, if I had a few free minutes to help her out with something. The next thing I knew, I was in a bear suit, milling around with nothing to do. I did manage to convince some young girls to sit on my lap for a photo op, and I was asked to join in one of the dances by another group of young and, I assume, fetching ladies. I can only assume for the same reason I had to decline; seeing out of the bear's eye holes was next to impossible, and I feared mayhem would ensue. The type that would not make good press.

But I came away from the event with the inner satisfaction of knowing that, for one brief, shining moment, I was Pudsey Bear. That, and a gift voucher to Ghyll Manor, which was how I came to be sitting in a swanky hotel having tea, cake and scones with clotted cream when I would usually be sitting on the balcony with a bottle of beer and a cigar. It was ever so civilized. Until I got to the scone.

It was full of raisins.

I can only conclude from this that they have outlawed plain scones sometime in the past five years when I wasn't paying attention. I had hoped, if a choice was offered, that they might have some real scones, but we didn't even get the option. I managed to swallow my disappointment (and the cake, and the scones, and the clotted cream as well as lots and lots of tea) and enjoy the day, but I am now more determined than ever to find "the lost scones of Britain."

Appropriately, I am now on a train heading to what may be the last bastion of truly civilized cream teas: Devon. I'm going out for work, but I will be staying there a few days each week over the next couple of months. This should provide ample time for me to get to know some of the local teashop owners and bakers and, you know, get the inside scoop on what is up with the raisins in the scones and, wink wink, oh, look, that twenty pound note just fell out of my pocket and into your hand, can you point me toward someplace where, um, a friend of mine can score some pure scone?

And he'll touch the side of his nose and lead me through the cobbled streets, past the thatching dens and into the dim alleys by the waterfront, to a seedy shop with boarded up windows and a peephole in the door under a crooked and weathered sign reading, "Ye Olde Tea Shoppe," where he'll knock a coded message and nod to the pair of eyes that peer out.

"He's all right," he'll say, and peephole will shut and door will creak open revealing a slice of yellow light.

I'll step in, the door will close and the cloaked figure will lead me through the dark halls into the back room where a few others are seated at mismatched tables and chairs with uneven legs.

A haggard matron will hand me a creased and dirty menu, and whisper, "We do the real thing here, honey; don't be shy, we know what you came for."

And I'll point to the menu and she'll nod and wink and slink into the darker reaches, returning with a silver tray containing a small jar of strawberry jam, a generous dollop of clotted cream and, in all its unadulterated glory, a plain scone. A low gasp will follow her across the room as the others gaze and sigh and she'll set it before me with a gleam in her watery eye.

116

"Can I have coffee with that," I'll ask. And she'll blanch and snatch away the tray.

"Get out, you pervert," she'll croak. "What sort of place do you think I'm running here?"

Krakow

Monday, Getting Started:

I've mentioned this before but it bears repeating: travel in the twenty-first century, despite its perceived difficulties, is far from the adventure it was in ages past. A hotel with only two stars and no tea-making amenities in the room cannot compare to hostile natives, malaria or sleeping on the ground with poisonous snakes and giant spiders.

As proof, here I am, in Poland, a place so foreign and remote and shrouded under the cloud or communism I thought it would be impossible for me to visit unless I somehow wangled a job as a spy, yet I'm being well looked after and everyone is kindly speaking to me in English (thereby avoiding the mutual embarrassment of me miming various phrases while speaking in loud, clearly enunciated syllables).

To get a real sense of travel excitement—where the accommodation is only marginally less dangerous than sleeping outside, the traditional cuisine is described as "imaginative" and the locals speak in an unintelligible language and seem just as likely to shower you with kindness as to slit your throat and steal your sunglasses—you need to go somewhere like Uzbekistan, rural Alabama or inner city Liverpool.

But I'm not that adventurous; I'm doing the "Captivating Cracow" tour with a reputable tour company and the only hardship I encountered while traveling was the unexpected lunacy of the airport requiring "every other person" to remove their shoes. This precipitated much shuffling about in the queue so the terrorists with the exploding Reeboks could sail through safely undetected.

And I have to give the security crew credit for being upbeat and chatty while they strip-searched my rucksack. Again. For some reason, the innocuous green backpack I have been carrying around for the past ten years elicits a disproportionate amount of suspicion, affording me the opportunity of meeting security officials at a variety of international airports. So far, Gatwick's staff have been the least thuggish and the most upbeat, and they win extra points for actually trying to convince me I wasn't under suspicion; they were just admiring my bag.

Aside from that, the three hour flight from London Gatwick to Krakow isn't a lot different than the three hour train ride from London Paddington to Totnes, except on the plane they bring you your food so you don't have to hike the equivalent of seven plane-lengths to buy it. And, of course, there remain the disturbing disparities in speed, altitude and the walk to the taxi rank once you arrive at your destination, but I prefer not to think about them.

Upon landing, we were herded into shuttle buses and driven—no exaggeration—about 100 yards to the terminal, where we were met by our tour guide, Janna (pronounced Ya' na). I knew she was Janna our tour guide because she said, "I'm Janna, I'll be your tour guide for the next five days whether you like it or not. Let's go out into the cold."

Janna is a tall, fetching young woman wearing the company uniform and sensible shoes (by which I mean nothing more than she walks a great deal in her job). Her dark hair is pulled back into a severe ponytail, which belies her mischievous nature and ready wit. She speaks better English than the girl at the local Costa Coffee and I wanted to ask her why she wasn't in Horsham screwing up my take-out order, but she beat me to it by trying to speak Polish to us on the bus ride to the hotel, then saying, "I thought you might have learned the language by now from all those Polish immigrants."

She's a bit of a comedienne, is our Janna.

Krakow, spelled and pronounced a variety of ways, is similar to the only other former Soviet Bloc city I have visited, meaning the ancient and lovely city center is surrounded by a ring of astonishingly ugly Communist architecture. But jarring juxtapositions seem the norm here.

The center is populated with upscale establishments in attractive buildings (some dating back as far as the 1300s) interspersed with kebab joints, money exchanges (whose dreary and foreboding storefronts make you think the exchange might possibly be only one way) and a variety of pizza restaurants. This afternoon's incessant drizzle served only to exacerbate the somberness of the surroundings and enhance my cold-war fantasies. Poland, I am sure, has some lovely weather—and a spot of sunshine would surely cheer the place up—but for now it looks like something out of a le Carré novel.

The people on these grey and dreary streets are well dressed, smiling, chatting on mobile phones and showing little ill effects of having been overrun by the Germans, the Germans,

119

the Communists and the EU. Mostly they look profitably busy and unconcerned with throwing off the shackles of Capitalism.

Our hotel, too, is a bit of a contradiction. It is, on the surface, elegant, but the structure harkens back to the Solid Block school of architecture, and our room looks to have been furnished with legacy Soviet-style IKEA products; sturdy and functional but austere. The features—a bed as comfortable as a queen-size prison cot with a single-size duvet, a flat-screen TV, a modern, if petite, bathroom, but no clock and no coffee-maker—combine to create a Spartan look and enhance the feeling that there ought to be more.

Incongruously, the bathroom, with its thin towels and miserly shower, is outfitted with the plushest toilet paper I have, literally, ever seen. Even the posh stuff at Waitrose isn't as soft or thick. They must have bought it on the black market.

Our only brush with the local culture occurred at the Loza Klub Aktora where we ducked in out of the rain for a cup of coffee. I am happy to report a lack—though, disappointingly, not a total absence—of American fast food restaurants in the city centre, which aided our resolve to brave the unfamiliar. The Loza turned out to be a rather posh affair, with art deco decor, lithe waitresses in skimpy black dresses and locals sipping coffee from tiny cups and smoking cigarettes.

Yes, smoking is still legal in Poland; I have even been informed that I can smoke a cigar in the hotel, though only in the downstairs lobby; all the rooms are non-smoking, even though there is an ashtray in mine. But in most bars, businesses and restaurants, no one will look askance at you for lighting up, or for much of anything, really.

This insouciance was put to the test when, just after we placed our order, a gaggle of people shuffled into the café. In the lead was a woman so skinny and eye-sunken she looked like death, followed by two normal, prettier lackeys and a camera crew. They entered, sat, ordered, ate, chatted and left, while the camera crew continued to film and hold a boom microphone over their heads. Not a soul in the place paid a blind bit of notice.

Because we're part of a group, we all sit down to dinner at the same time, and we have a "set" menu, which means you eat what they put in front of you. Oddly, the vegetarian meal of potato perogies they whipped up for my wife was more traditional than the normal meal, which was simply meat and mashed potatoes.

During the meal, we became better acquainted with the other members of our group and I learned, if you are ever in the company of a lot of British people and the conversation lags, mention rubbish collection and you're home free.

Just one more observation before retiring to our medium-sized bed and small-sized duvet: around town, I noticed a lot of signs in English, yet there is no large English population here. While I am grateful for being able to understand the locals and freely admit that Polish is well beyond my abilities, I am conscious of the uproar that ensues when signs appear in New York with Spanish translations. But they don't seem to harbor that prejudice here.

And in closing, allow me to point out that just because there are a lot of English translations here doesn't mean they are all that good at it, unless the "well educated" mushrooms I had at dinner really did go to Cambridge.

Tuesday, The Salt Mine:

After a few hours of wrestling for the duvet, we flipped a zloty for it; my wife won, so I had to wrap up in the bedspread. For all that, it wasn't the worst night I have ever spent in a hotel and, even if I was a bit fatigued, the morning shower grabbed my full attention. It was, to all appearances, a normal, innocuous shower, but with most of the shower jets clogged up with sediment, the three or four working ones shot the water out with a force that could bore a hole through solid lead; they certainly did a fair job on my aching body.

They also have the standard "save the planet by not making us replace your towels every day" scheme here, and like everywhere else, they replace the towels daily whether you want them to or not. (I marked them; I have proof.)

Breakfast was typically continental—rolls, meats, cheeses, cereals, yogurt, really, really strong coffee and some lukewarm water and herbal tea bags. My guess: this is a "coffee" country. Also, I've grown tired of the "liquid nitrogen" joke (that's what I always accuse the kitchen staff of storing their butter in), so I snagged a couple of butter packets from breakfast so I could thaw them out in my room and use them during the week.

The morning was taken up with a tour of the city, which is compact, accessible and charming, especially on a crisp, cold morning. It's also a very clean city. I was just as impressed with the tidy streets—clear of kebab wrappers, empty crisp packets, polka dots of disused gum and dog doo—as I was with the buildings. They seem to take a lot of pride in their city, which the British have managed to avoid. Perhaps this is because, if you have a country that, for large swaths of time throughout history, did not exist, you value it more when it is there.

Krakow was overlooked in the WWII bombing runs so many of its building are very old, especially in the Jewish Quarter. This is where Herr Schindler had his factory and composed his famous List. It's a sign of the times that, years ago, they used to point this out by saying, "Schindler's factory was here," whereas now they say, "*Schindler's List* was filmed here."

After the tour, we stopped to listen to the bugler in the tower. Some years back (a lot of them) when the Tartars had a habit of attacking the city, a bugler would watch from the tower and sound the call to arms when he saw the marauders approaching. On this particular day, when he was about eight bars into his serenade, he was struck in the throat by an arrow. The music suddenly stopped, but the legend lives on because Don McLean wrote about the day the music died, (no, that was about Buddy Holly and his ill-fated encounter with gravity); the legend lives on because every hour, on the hour, twenty four hours a day, seven days a week, the bugle sounds from the tower window and abruptly stops at the point where the hapless bugler was delivered an extreme critique. Or at least that's the story. Volunteers man the bugle post (yes, it's a real person, not a recording) and it's considered a bit of an honor to be able to get up at 3 o'clock on Saturday morning to play eight bars of bugle music to an empty square. And the bugle call sounds more like a dirge than an alarm; if the real watchman was playing that tune, he wouldn't have roused the city to arms, he would have put them to sleep.

After that bit of street theatre, we found a café, enjoyed a light lunch, a nice sit down and a cigar (well, I enjoyed the cigar, at any rate). It was strange to be allowed to smoke inside and the waitress was surprised when I asked if it was okay. It was also surprising that we were allowed to sit, unmolested by the staff who, in the US, would be stopping at our table every five minutes to see if we wanted anything else to eat or drink and, if not, then why were we still sitting there. I just wonder how long it will last.

The EU will soon put paid to that, both the sitting and my smoking. And then they'll regulate the pretzel vendors out of business, and health and safety will force the bugler to stop bugling, and the market square will be cordoned off because the cobbles are uneven and perogies will be limited to a specific region near the Czech boarder and then we'll all be safe when we visit Krakow, except it won't be Krakow any longer, it will be just another location, indistinguishable from Paris, or London, or Prague or any other EU-ravaged city, where you can sit in inoffensive safety while you eat your Big Mac, drink your Starbuck's coffee and hit the road as soon as you finish. But that's just my opinion; for now, I'll content myself with enjoying Krakow while I am still allowed to.

When the bill came, I checked it so I could calculate the tip but found I couldn't read any of the items. The numbers made sense, but what we were paying for remained a mystery. After a few attempts, I gave up and started counting out money to match the final amount on the bill, which turned out to be the time. My wife eventually located the proper price, I calculated the tip and we left for the salt mine.

The weather for "Salt Mine Day" could not have turned out better; in the morning, during the tour, it was cold and crisp, and in the afternoon, while we were down in the mine, it was sleeting and miserable. By the time we got back to ground level, it was sunny again.

And while those above ground were enduring a less than ideal afternoon, we were treated to one of the most unique and awesome visual experience I have been privileged to witness.

There are only three kilometers of mine included in the tour. The total length of the mine, if stretched out straight, would be 300 kilometers. And there are sculptures in every part of it. The miners did not carve them for tourists to gawp at; they were a religious and superstitious (not to mention talented) lot, and did the carvings for their own satisfaction and use. Many of them are little chapels where they prayed and held services. One magnificent sculpture was of a queen who had something, along with her wedding ring, to do with Lithuania. I'm sorry, I was too busy enjoying the artwork to pay full attention to the narrative; I didn't know there was going to be a quiz afterward so I didn't take notes.

The sculptures are not actually made of salt, but of the soft rock that the salt is extracted from. The mine has been in nearly continuous operation for hundreds of years and, in its heyday, provided 25% of the nation's wealth. It has now ceased production, but the sculptures the miners left behind pull in over a million visitors a year, and that's a lot of zlotys. There's a nice symmetry in that.

In one section of the tunnel, there was a tableau depicting how the miners worked, though the figures looked more like Dopey, Sleepy and their friends than Polish miners. It makes sense; now that their brief movie career is over they were probably glad for the gig.

The tour culminated in The Chapel, which was more of a cathedral. It was impossibly immense and ornate, and very far underground. Even so, they actually hold proper church services there. And every bit of it—the tiled floor, the altar, the portraits of the saints, the chandeliers, the huge rendering of Da Vinci's Last Supper—was carved from the salt rock by the miners.

Also in the mine are networks of immense wooden girders holding up the ceilings. It was quite a feat of engineering just getting the wood down here, never mind erecting these massive and intricate support structures. In one corner of the chapel I found a statue dedicated to the carpenters; a tribute to the craftsmen who kept the mine roof from landing on their heads.

No tour is complete without a visit to the Gift Shoppe and the Café. It's the same here, but with a twist. The Gift Shoppe is several hundred meters underground, and just a short walk down a corridor carved through the rock, is the café. And there, surrounded by all this salty, subterranean opulence, made possible by countless hours of dedicated carving by generations of artistic miners, I had a beer and a bag of peanut M&Ms.

Wednesday, The Death Camp:

The morning of our trip to Auschwitz we woke up to snow. In Britain, the tour would have been canceled along with our flight home on Friday, but in Krakow, it wasn't even mentioned. I was a bit disappointed; I had been looking forward to seeing Auschwitz in all its desolate glory, but covered in a fresh blanket of snow, it might appear as picturesque as a fairy land. I needn't have worried.

As the bus pulled out of Krakow toward the camps, Janna explained what to expect. Rather jarringly, the combination of her accent and perky travel-rep persona had her reeling off the day's offerings as if we were on our way to a theme park:

"You'll see the barracks where the prisoners were held, the execution wall, the gas chambers, the crematoriums…" But then she added: "We won't stay there long; you might become suicidal."

To lighten the mood, she then treated us to a Polish lesson, which we all failed miserably. And any enthusiasm I had for attempting the local language was quelled when she told us the word for "Thank you" and "Pig" sounded nearly identical.

Janna, it turns out, is Czech, but she also speaks Polish, Russian, English and some Italian and French. This makes my failure to learn "Thank you" (or even "Pig") in Polish abysmally pathetic by comparison, even if she occasionally finds being multi-lingual problematic: after our lesson, Janna told us: "We will be riding an hour and a half, so you may take off your clothes. I mean coats." But I think she mostly does this on purpose.

It's strange, but whenever I'm in Europe, and particularly Eastern Europe, I tend to take in the landscape while imaging how it must have appeared with the armies of one nation or another advancing over it, or how it felt to be under the somber and unseen, but palpable, weight of Communist domination. I can't help it; this is what I was brought up believing, and a trip to Auschwitz wasn't about to do much to dispel that, even if I was arriving on a heated bus instead of an overcrowded cattle-car.

Auschwitz, it seems to me, is the antithesis of the Anne Frank House (which I also recommend); it provides a way to connect, but at different ends of the scale. You can't mourn for the unnamed and untold number of those who died in the war, but you can mourn for one little girl whose story makes her as real to you as your own daughter, or sister, or niece, and you can mourn for the millions—though many remain unnamed and unnumbered—murdered in a single location if you are able to see the place where it happened. That's what Auschwitz does, it reminds us, by brute force, not to forget.

Upon our arrival, we were checked in, directed to a darkened room and told to wait. I wondered if this was their method of getting us in the mood and if we were going to be treated to a pretend shower. Instead, they showed us a cheesy Soviet-era reenactment of the liberation of the camp. It was not an auspicious beginning; I would have preferred the shower.

The crimes of Auschwitz have grown to mythic proportions, and that's a shame, because what happened there was horrific enough without attempting to enhance it. Like many others, I have a fairly solid idea of what the Nazis (those not busy chasing Steve McQueen and his motorcycle around the countryside or trying to stop the Von Trapp family from opening a ski lodge in Vermont, at any rate) were up to in the early 1940s:

- First, they decided the path to a utopian society required killing all the Jews.

125

- Then they built Auschwitz, Dachau, Treblinka and other camps to see this idea to fruition.
- Though the camps operated at full tilt up until they were liberated, the Germans fell short of their goal, and have been the butt of jokes—such as the one speculating on the seating capacity of their microwave ovens—ever since.

Based on what Tasia, our guide, told us over the course of our tour, every bit of that is wrong, except the part about the oven jokes:

- When people say "Auschwitz," they mean Birkenau, which was the actual extermination camp.
- When people say Birkenau, they actually mean Brzezinka, which was what the nearby town—from where the camp took its name—was called until the Nazis renamed it in 1939. Auschwitz used to be known as Oswiecim.
- Auschwitz, the concentration camp, was already there; it had been a barracks for the Polish army, built in 1918 after gaining their independence in the First World War. The Germans merely converted it to hold prisoners. The camp was opened for business on 14 June 1940. It housed mostly Polish prisoners.
- After the Final Solution was conceived and authorized, it was tested and perfected at Auschwitz. When that camp became over crowded, the prisoners were forced to build Birkenau. Birkenau had the infamous showers.
- It was the showers that were the unique feature of the extermination camps, not the crematoriums. Other camps had crematoriums, as well, to keep up with the bodies of prisoners who died of natural causes, if you can call being stripped, starved, tortured and worked to death in appalling conditions "natural".
- The aim of the Final Solution was to rid the world of Jews, Gypsies and Poles; the Nazis were nothing if not ambitious.
- Auschwitz/Birkenau was chosen because it had good rail links and was isolated. Six villages were evacuated and loyal Germans were moved into the surrounding area in order to keep the secret.
- Despite these precautions, the Allies did know about the exterminations, but the camp was too far away for them to reach. The Americans refused to bomb the

railway lines because the accuracy of the bombs at that time would make it ineffective.

- Promises of land and work opportunities were used to trick Jews and other so-called undesirables into allowing themselves to be deported to Auschwitz from Czechoslovakia, Poland, Italy, Greece and as far away as Norway.
- The prisoners were taken directly from the trains to the showers, gassed and cremated. They only designated a few of them for work purposes, though as time went on they chose more and more for work details.
- There were other camps operating to bring about The Final Solution. Treblinka, Sobibor, Belzec were extermination camps only; inmates were brought in and immediately executed. Two others extermination centers, Chelmno and Majdanek operated as concentration camps as well. These camps were smaller than Auschwitz/Birkenau and were dismantled in 1943/44. Operations were then consolidated at Auschwitz/Birkenau.
- Being sent to a camp—execution or not—was practically a certain death sentence. The average life expectancy for men was 8 to 12 months; for women it was 3 to 4 months.
- And one final, shocking truth (in case you still harbor some grudging admiration for the Nazis): of the 1.5 million people murdered by the Nazis in Auschwitz/Birkenau, 20% were children.

In late 1944 the Germans knew they were losing the war and set about dismantling Auschwitz. The first thing they did was try to murder all the prisoners they had forced to help them. They took one hundred of them from Birkenau to Auschwitz and gassed them there, but the crematorium at Auschwitz had been turned into an armory after the construction of Birkenau, so they sent the bodies back to Birkenau for cremation where they were recognized by the other prisoners. When the Nazis tried to select the next lot of prisoners for execution, they rebelled and managed to blow up one of the crematoriums. The rebels were rounded up and killed. The other ovens and death chambers were blown up and the camp abandoned. The Nazis took 100,000 prisoners with them to other work camps in Germany and left 700,000 to fend for themselves.

In January 1945 the camp was liberated by a Ukrainian unit of the Russian Army.

The famous sign, *"Arbeit macht frei"*—Work Makes You Free—was constructed by inmates skilled in metal working. It still hangs over the entrance to Auschwitz.

Thursday, Zakopane:

Zak' o pan; it sounds more like something out of Babylon 5 or Star Trek than a quaint mountain village ("Ensign Xapazork, we've just entered the Zakopane System, commence scanning for Zakopannian warships and the buxom Zakobabes who pilot them." "Aye, Captain! Communicating with them on our wall-sized, high-definition monitors will do wonders for our ratings, especially if we catch them during molting season.")

It seemed the further south we traveled the colder and snowier it became. Back in West Sussex, the tulips were beginning to bud; in Krakow, the first crocuses were just starting to peek through the soil, and as we traveled to Zakopane, we entered a region blanketed in deep snow. Makes me wonder when spring arrives here.

My reverie was broken by Janna, who eagerly filled us in on the local knowledge:

"Has anyone been to Zakopane before? You have? Ah, that's too bad, I was gonna make stuff up."

Once again, the terrain reminded me vaguely of America. In the open countryside, the wind and the fresh snowfall combined to raise wintry whirlwinds. The roads were straight, the fields long and flat, the towns a mish-mash of housing styles grouped around a general store and auto dealerships. Billboards cluttered up the roadside spoiling the scenery; no fetching country lanes here, it looked more like an American side street.

But as we headed higher into the mountains, the snow deepened, the forest grew thick and the billboards fell behind. Pope John Paul II was born not far away and spent a good deal of time skiing and hiking in the Zakopane region, so the locals claim him as their own. Statues of His holiness abound and, as you might expect, a large and impressive church was constructed as thanks to God for sparing him in the 1981 assassination attempt.

We exited the bus into more snow than most of the group had ever seen in a lifetime, or about as much as I used to see in the average February. Our local guide is a young lady named Aga, who narrated the tour even though Janna spoke better

English and knew the area every bit as well. It must be a holdover from communism's full-employment philosophy.

Aga told us that Zakopane (actually pronounced Zak o PAN' a) means "Hidden." The area boast only 30,000 year-round inhabitants but Zakopane and the surrounding mountains are visited each year by 6 million tourists. The area is popular with hikers, mountain climbers, ski enthusiasts and others who just enjoy the history or the fresh air. Zakopane is different from rest of Poland. The houses are spectacular wooden structures especially designed to withstand the heavy snow. The tourist industry was alive there as long ago as the 17th century, when painters and artists came to draw inspiration from the surrounding mountains. They were followed by the nobles and soon Zakopane became the place to be.

And did you know that Pope John Paul II was from this area? Just go for a visit; they won't let you forget it.

On the way back to the bus, I asked Aga what other businesses were in the area besides tourism. She said, "There is no other business; shops, hotels, skiing—they all depends on tourists." I had to admire her candor.

We were then bussed into Zakopane proper for some free time and a look around the "quaint" old village. As we wandered along the ironically named pedestrian area, I saw more US fast food franchises in one block than in all of Krakow. Later, we had lunch at a theme restaurant and took a quick tour through the famous outdoor market that, despite its impressive size, managed to avoid offering—even by accident—a single useful item.

On the long ride back to Krakow, Janna told us more about storks than I thought there was to know. And believe it or not, it was fascinating, but once again I forgot to take notes. And not only does she know more than is healthy about storks, she's also a budding comedian: "People ask me if I'm gonna get married. I tell dem I get nervous if I have milk in the fridge for a week."

Thanks for a memorable week, Janna.

Janna and the Communists

As a young boy, the only thing I knew about the Communists was that they were trying to kill me. When the air raid sirens sounded, I would scurry indoors to wait for the all clear, or for the bombs to start falling. If the latter happened, I knew that meant The End, and although I don't recall anyone saying this out loud, I was pretty sure it was all the Communist's fault.

For much of my life, a good deal of real estate was locked behind the Iron Curtain, and what little I knew about life on the other side was gleaned from John le Carré novels and films, such as *White Nights*. Thus, when I first found myself on ex-Soviet soil, I became intensely interested about what life had been like before the KFC franchises arrived. Asking a local, without first buying him several shots of slivovice, would have been in bad taste, so I had to quell my curiosity and settle for sightseeing instead.

But on this, my second excursion into the erstwhile Evil Empire, during the long bus ride back to Krakow from Zakopane, Janna, after finishing her soliloquy on storks, told us her story of growing up under Communism. The following is compiled from the notes I scribbled as she spoke and I hope I have reassembled them in a coherent order:

Janna is from Prague in the Czech Republic, which was Czechoslovakia when she was born. Communism began there in 1948 and lasted 41 years. Janna was born in 1978; she was 11 when it ended.

Having been born into it, life under the Communist regime simply seemed normal. It wasn't slavery, it was just putting up with restrictions and fewer options, and since they knew nothing else, there was no reason to be jealous. "Money was not important," she told us, "we were all equally poor." The advantages they enjoyed included (ostensibly) no homelessness or unemployment. The government gave you a job. All salaries for similar work were the same so no one had more than anyone else. The government provided you with a place to live. You shopped at the local market. Life went on.

In Janna's world, the government owned everything— shops, schools, businesses—and you were not allowed to work part-time or start your own business. The government flats were small and drab with a kitchen she described as "being so small you could sit in the middle and cook with one hand and wash the dishes with the other." (Recall that Janna is a budding comedienne—there may be a bit of comic exaggeration in there.)

In school, they learned the national language—Russian. They studied Russian literature, they read Russian poets. Learning English was forbidden and no western books were available. The only western books allowed were those that showed the bad side of society, like *Oliver Twist*. When she was eight, her class was shown a documentary about a typical British family. The father was an alcoholic, the mother a prostitute. They beat their children and lived in poverty. (Yes, I realize it sounds like a council estate in Liverpool, but that's not the point.) The class took up a collection to send to the poor children in England. They had hoped to receive a "Thank You" in return, but none ever came.

Religion was not forbidden, but you had to be careful. If someone saw you in church you could be punished. Back in the 1950's, you could go to prison for a short while but later you were simply denied promotions and your children might be barred from entering the university. How she thinks this means it wasn't forbidden is a mystery; perhaps, if you weren't simply taken out and shot, that meant it was okay.

During Communism, the shops were not empty; they just didn't offer a choice. You queued for bread, butter, milk and it was all the same brand. Everything was purchased from the local market. When you went to the shop, you bought what you could get. If you went for potatoes, you might have to buy rice instead or they might tell you to try again in a few weeks. If you saw people queuing you joined them because you knew they were selling something good. And if you found an item you wanted to buy, you had to buy other goods in order to get it. Some items you had to be put on a list for, and it could take years to get a TV or a fridge.

They were allowed to travel, but only to other Soviet controlled countries, and they were not allowed to bring any items back with them. So when they went on holiday, they would wear old shoes, throw them away and buy new ones. If they bought sausages they would gnaw the ends off in the hopes the guards would not confiscate them. When they visited a region in Poland renowned for lace curtains, they wore loose clothing and wrapped the curtains around themselves under their clothing.

In the 1980s, some people decided they had had enough. Strikes were called by the universities, students, writers, poets and artists. They wanted democracy and, under pressure, the government eventually stepped down. For Janna, it was an easy transition; being on the cusp of her life, she suddenly saw a whole new and exciting world open up for her. People in her mother's generation were mostly glad for the change but found it difficult to come to grips with the new order. They had to learn a new language and new technology but, in time, they caught on. For the people in her grandmother's generation, it was very hard. Everything they had believed in, everything they had known and a lifetime of the government taking care of them was suddenly gone. They suffered the most.

Overnight, it seemed, there were new buildings, shopping centers, cinemas, Levis jeans and Coca Cola. And everything cost 300% more than what it used to.

English began to be taught in schools and the teachers were often only one lesson ahead of their pupils.

Travel was now possible. New learning. More choices. Janna went to London to study, and her current career would have been unthinkable under Communism.

Communism only worked as long as the government could keep its people from finding out what the alternative was. Once they found out, they wanted it, and now there is no going back. They have gained a great deal but, in Janna's view, what they have lost is the sense of community.

"We helped each other under Communism. If someone ran out of milk or beer, we helped them; we lived like one big family. Now people aren't so neighborly."

And life goes on.

For Whom the Dinner Bell Tolls

It was a cool but clear morning and I was on my way to visit a client in a pleasant little village just beginning to succumb to the clawing spread of the megalopolis that is London. I was looking forward to a relaxing breakfast and a productive day, and I had no idea life was about to take an instant and irrevocable turn for the worse.

The town associated with this particular client in has a cafe right next to their offices. This is a proper, working man's cafe (pronounced Kaff), not a café, which is pronounced ka-FAY and is a different thing altogether. It's a wonderful place, dim yet inviting, with a comfortably worn linoleum floor and a cluttered counter where the specials are hand-written and fixed to the side of the cash register with yellowed cellophane tape. An elderly man in an equally elderly apron runs the place, and after just two sporadic visits, he began greeting my arrival with, "The number two with no sausage and extra bacon, right?" He would then call the order to the affable woman at the grill while I took a seat at one of the large, round tables scattered randomly throughout the room.

They would bring the coffee (fresh brewed, hot and strong), toast and then my breakfast, but the table was large enough to spread out my papers and laptop and, after eating, I was always able to get a bit of work done and enjoy a second cup of coffee before heading to the client's offices.

And on this morning, while looking forward to this treat, I began thinking how ephemeral these types of experiences are becoming; authentic encounters with real people in real places. Genuine cafes, pubs, village shops—they are all becoming a thing of the past and I was grateful for finding this one before it joined Woolworth's in that great Chapter 11 in the sky.

I won't say I had a premonition or anything, it was more of Sod's Law in action, but when I came in sight of the cafe and saw the spiffy, yellow canopy and sparkling metal tables with matching chairs in the sidewalk seating area, I knew my treasured find had become yet another casualty to the relentless march of progress.

Inside, a faux wooden floor gleamed under the glare of florescent lights and the age-darkened walls were now dazzlingly bright and adorned with mass-produced artwork. The venerable counter and kitchen area had been completely rebuilt and, in the process, the congenial couple had been replaced by a bevy of chatty teenagers with red and black uniforms, paper hats and foreign accents. A desperately cheerful, illuminated menu board hung over a backlit display case filled with pastries and soft drinks, and the counter where I was apparently expected to place my order looked as inviting as the service desk at the Department of Motor Vehicles (that's the DVLA to you people on this side of the Atlantic).

After some confusion regarding the ordering protocol, I took a seat at one of the fast-food-orange Formica tables neatly gridded in the dining area. Although the table was surrounded by four matching chairs (complete with padded plastic seats in an eye-watering shade of crimson), I had barely enough room to put my notebook and laptop without having to disturb the neat row of condiments and the garish, laminated menu.

An apathetic waitress brought my coffee; it was the best instant coffee money could buy, lukewarm and over-milked. When my breakfast arrived, I packed up my gear because there was no room for the plate. I had ordered a simple meal of fried eggs and bacon, thinking that would be difficult to cock up, but the eggs were suspiciously uniform in shape, leading me to believe they were mass-produced at a processing plant in Leeds, flash frozen and sent down by Royal Mail so these teenagers could heat them up. And that's what they tasted like, as well. I don't remember the bacon, which speaks volumes on its own.

I hastened through my breakfast—this was not a place that encouraged lingering over a meal—and headed to my client's offices, feeling a growing tinge of sadness that yet another bit of old Britain had been brushed away and replaced by American-style sizzle with no substance.

People nowadays don't want to savor a well-cooked meal in congenial surroundings, they want garish colors and fast food; and they don't seek conversation and a pint in a quiet pub, they'd rather have deafening music, flashing lights and drinks the color of toilet bowl cleaner. That's the reality, that's progress, and there's no stopping it.

That doesn't mean I have to like it, but it does mean I have to find another cafe.

Tales of the Road

Traveling for work again, but I won't mention the town in case someone who lives there reads this.

Now, I'm an oddity, even by British standards; I like to travel by public transport and, a country boy at heart, I look forward to staying in small towns; the smaller the better. So buoyed by my recent visits to Devon and my erstwhile journeys to rural Wales, I looked forward to visiting this new part of the country and experiencing a bit of the local life.

I should have known I was in for some surprises when I arrived at the station and found, just as the lady at the hotel assured me I would, an abundance of taxis, but not a single driver. They were parked in a long row outside of the station, each one of them empty. After the three people who got off the train with me dispersed, I found myself alone. So I wandered the parking lot in circles, as I do when I am uncertain, trying to decide which way would lead me to the town center. I selected a route at random and, by asking directions three times, found the high street and my hotel.

To be kind, it reminded me of my favorite hotel in Llandrindod Wells, a venerable structure of faded Victorian glory, only this hotel wasn't Victorian and, though faded, it had no glory, past or present. I found my room in a separate building that I appeared to have to myself, which struck me as odd and a bit unkind. Why, if all the other rooms were empty, did they stick me in the room with the buzz?

It wasn't horribly loud, but it was annoying, unending and stubbornly mysterious. I patrolled the room, checked the closet, looked in the bathroom and put my ear up to the heater. Was it louder here, or there? I tried the lights, flicked switches, nothing made it stop. I gave up and unpacked.

My room had a retractable TV stand, but the television had gone walkabout, along with all the hangers. In their place, a mismatched array of hangers lifted from a local bargain store hung on the railing, alongside the hooks for the theft-resistance hangers. Apparently, they had encountered a thief who enjoyed a challenge. Whoever it was also stole the plug for the bathtub. The replacement plug was not attached to the chain, which made it—as I discovered after my bath the next morning—impossible to extract from the drain.

There was a coffee pot, but no place to plug it in so I set it on the TV stand and used the TV's vacant socket. Then I washed my hands and found the source of the buzz; it was the cold-water faucet in the bathroom.

The faucet ran constantly and, try as I might, I could only slow the water to a trickle, which merely raised the pitch of the buzz. The mystery was solved, but the problem remained; with no other course of action open to me, I went into town to hunt down dinner.

I had high hopes of finding a nice, traditional pub with a beer garden where I could have a pub meal, a few pints, a cigar or two and some discourse with the locals. Instead I found kebab joints, fried chicken emporiums and a startling number of youths in hooded jackets milling around in alleyways. I walked up one side of the street and down the other and am pretty sure I took in all the town had to offer. There were pubs, but not the type I was looking for, and before I even started back toward my hotel, I knew I wasn't going to find any, just as I knew, if I looked in the local phone directory, I wouldn't find an over-abundance of last names.

Given this, I was surprised to discover that my hotel had a restaurant, and a liquor license. They also had a spacious deck with a view overlooking the graveyard, so I had hopes that the neighbors, at least, would be quiet because my room certainly wasn't. I retired early to get some work done but the incessant buzzing was so distracting I couldn't concentrate. After an hour I gave up and, without much hope, went to bed.

I tried everything I could to block the noise, but the quieter the night became the louder droned the buzz. So I got up at 5:30, only to discover there was no way to take a shower. The bathroom contained an ample bathtub but merely a showerhead on a handle, which would do me little good. It wasn't that I minded getting the bathroom carpet all wet (rule of thumb: carpet in bathroom, hotel not up to par) but I couldn't imagine trying to shampoo my hair while holding a live showerhead in one hand. In the end I took a bath, something that, as an American, I am not very keen on. A shower energizes you and gets you moving, a bath can put you to sleep, as mine almost did, even as the buzzing rang in my ears.

After breakfast, shaved and suited, I wheeled my suitcase out the door and flicked off the light for the last time. The buzzing stopped.

I waited; sure it would start back up again. It didn't. Fearing I was suffering from lack of sleep and hallucinating this perfect ending to my tale, I went back into the room. I turned on lights, flicked switches, ran the faucets. Nothing. Just blissful, belated silence.

I left the room, the hotel and the town. I will not be back.

Blame It On the Railroad

Where British trains are concerned, it is a truth universally acknowledged, at least by myself, that no matter how much time I leave myself, I will never make a train connection in London where I board my train not in a sweat or a state of panic, or both.

This time, for once, I thought I had it sussed. First of all, I wasn't going to London, I was only going as far as Reading. Second, I had 47 minutes between trains, and after a long hot day at work and a two and a half hour ride on a standing-room-only train, I was looking forward to sitting quietly in the corner of the station, reading my book and maybe enjoying a packet of salt-and-vinegar crisps for dinner. When traveling by train, it is best to keep your expectations low; I didn't try hard enough.

Soon after we entered Hampshire, we began making random and unexplained stops. Time after time the train ground to a halt and we would peer through the windows expecting to see a station and seeing, instead, sheep and pastureland. We would admire the view for a while, the driver would apologize for the delay and the train would clank and wheeze and start to roll again. A few pastures later, we would find ourselves, once again, stationary and staring at sheep. The only theory I can come up with is that the train driver was a keen photographer and felt the need to stop every five minutes so he could take pictures of the fetching landscape.

As the minutes ticked by, more and more of my fellow passengers began calling ahead for alternative transportation. But I still had 20 minutes—no, make that 17 minutes—to go. I could still make it.

We managed to roll into Reading station just 40 minutes late (pretty good by British standards) leaving me seven minutes to locate my train in a large and unfamiliar station.

As is my habit when I'm late, I rushed around in circles looking for my platform and, by sheer accident, discovered an escalator that would take me upstairs where I could, hopefully, find another escalator to take me down to my train.

Surprisingly, at this point, I still had four minutes. What could possibly go wrong? I piled onto the escalator, and pulled my suitcase up behind me, crammed in with all the other folks rushing because they, too, were late. In front of me was a guy with either a very large guitar case or a cello. As the flat bit of the escalator rose into steps, the angle of the case changed and it began to press against me—first my knees, then my waist— while at the same time, my suitcase stopped supporting me by my waist and lowered itself to my knee level.

I knew falling was inevitable, but there was little to hang on to and, besides, I had a briefcase in one hand and a suitcase in the other; if I let go of either one to grab the handrail, the luggage would roll down the escalator. Before it twigged that the alternative meant I, as well as my luggage, would end up rolling down the escalator, we were already doing it.

For an unrehearsed performance, I pulled off one spectacular fall. I careened off half a dozen people on the way down, which was remarkably far because the bottom of the stairway kept getting lower. And then, when my back finally met the steps, I, and my luggage, kept sliding downward. I came to rest near the bottom, amid a small crowd of astonished commuters, with my briefcase lying on my chest. I have been in more comfortable positions, but at least I had stopped moving.

"Are you all right?" someone asked.

I assured them I was.

"Do you want help getting up?"

With my head pointing downward, I couldn't imagine scrambling upright on a crowded, moving escalator, so I said:

"No, thanks. I'll just lie here until we reach the top."

And I did.

To my everlasting regret, it was only in retrospect that I remembered I have been waiting for just such an opportunity so I could scream:

"Oh my God! I'm hurt! Somebody call a lawyer!"

Instead, I just lay there peacefully staring up at the startled faces staring down at me. At the top, some helpful commuters found my suitcase while two others pulled me to my feet as I slid onto the floor of the upper deck.

I thanked them profusely, but then wondered if, this being Britain, I should have apologized for inconveniencing them, instead. No matter. I made it to my train, in a sweat and a panic, with seconds to spare and my lawyer joke, along with my truth universally acknowledged, stowed safely away for another day.

America—From Both Sides Now

Despite the hassles of getting in, I always enjoy visiting America and rediscovering wide roads, open spaces and bottles of aspirin with more than 12 pills inside. This trip was different in that I wasn't going home; we zipped through Albany—staying just long enough to show it to my in-laws, which took about 20 minutes—en route to Syracuse to witness The Boy take his initial step into the land of indentured servit- Ouch! Cut that out! Yes, dear: I mean, marital bliss.

It was great to drive though the Land of Bumper Stickers, where I could get Half and Half for my coffee and eat in restaurants where, if they didn't bring your food within ten minutes, they came and apologized, sometimes bringing free goodies in the bargain. (For the sake of balance: while dining at a Friendly's Restaurant, after assuring our theretofore obsequious waitress that we didn't want dessert, she was Johnny-on-the-spot with our bill and the implicit message, "If you're not paying, you're not staying.")

Common sense seems to be even less popular in the US than it is in Britain, as witnessed by the fact that my old swimming hole had a "No swimming while lifeguard is not on duty" sign prominently displayed. A lifeguard? At a bend in the creek? Have children grown so stupid that they need 24-hour coddling?

It seems so, because a large and incongruously picturesque fountain in Syracuse (if you've been to Syracuse, you'll understand why it was so incongruous) had an even larger barrier surrounding it, apparently to keep people from drowning in the six inches of water in the fountain pool.

It was also sad to see the government so hopelessly inept at meaningful security. It seems they must have read (and possibly contributed to) the *Cowering in Your Homeland; a Guide to Over-Reaction* manual because, when we went to visit the observation deck in the Corning Tower, the security we found in place was madness at its best.

If you're afraid that someone is trying to blow up your building, you check the people coming in by looking in their bags, making them walk through a scanner or insisting they leave their firearms with the hat-check girl on the ground floor. If they have no weapons or explosive devices (and aren't suspiciously swarthy) you let them through. But that's not good enough for Albany.

We had to show photo ID: no ID, no observation deck. Fortunately, we all had something with our picture on it. The couple behind us did not, so they were turned away as obvious terrorists and denied a view of the Hudson Valley from above. We, on the other hand, having established we could laminate a photo of ourselves over a random piece of identification, were allowed through. We were then photographed and a cheesy, photocopy-quality sticker was produced, which we had to wear during the visit. After that we were allowed up.

During this entire process I was carrying a rucksack and my wife had a suspiciously bulging handbag, but no one even looked at them. That's not security, that's just paranoia turned into meaningless action masquerading as security.

But that's just the government embracing the absurd, as governments are wont to do. What really made me lose heart was the sight of a young man in a coffee shop who, after moving a beverage machine so he could plug in his laptop, spent a good five minutes arranging his gadgets, booting up and opening programs in order to play solitaire. Have we become so divorced from common sense that we don't even know how to operate a deck of cards anymore? It makes me want to weep.

To my eternal relief, moments such as these were few, and most of our American adventures were decidedly upbeat, even our encounter with the rabid woodchuck.

My wife, being from England, is unfamiliar with both woodchucks and rabies and was, therefore, unprepared for a face-to-face with this fellow. Seeing as how he was mangy, apparently confused, aggressive, and blocking the path in front of us, I took a cautious view and gave him a wide berth. I then notified a park ranger but it turns out we had simply stumbled upon the rodent equivalent of a grumpy old man sitting on his porch screaming at the neighborhood kids.

"They have no natural predators here," the ranger told me. "He's just old and cranky."

The culmination of the trip was the wedding. But before we get to the "Awwww" moment, I need to mention, once again, the amazing hospitality, friendliness, helpfulness and overall

141

kindness of the American people (and I am not leaving out our cordial neighbors to the north, who are even more ready than people in the US to strike up conversations with complete strangers). We see so much of the bad side of America on the news that we start to believe they are all war-mongering fundamentalist fanatics, and nothing could be further from the truth, as my wife's trip to the emergency room demonstrated:

As a direct result of visiting the park (as well as other encounters with nature) my wife collected an impressive array of bumps, rashes and swollen areas. The day before the wedding, these reached critical mass and it became suddenly apparent that she needed medical aid. I was in an unfamiliar town with no way to contact anyone, but the clerk at the store we were in allowed me to use their phone. I called my son, who told me to go to his fiancée's house. At the house, we were met by her father who jumped in his car and led us to an emergency clinic.

Once it became clear that they would actually see my wife instead of sending her out to die by the roadside with all the other uninsured people, I told the father of the bride that he could leave us to it. This was, after all, probably a very busy day for him and I was amazed that he even had time to show us to the clinic. But he wouldn't have it. Not only that, in the five minutes we had in the waiting room before my wife was called in, the entire family—including the bride—showed up. They didn't need to be there, we weren't expecting them to come and they had every reason to be elsewhere, but they were genuinely concerned and wanted to make sure we were all right. They stayed—chatting with my in-laws while my wife was being seen to and I acted as her interpreter—and wouldn't leave until she was pronounced non-terminal (turns out she's allergic to North America) and provided with effective medication.

The best thing to come out of this incident, of course, is that now we have a Rite-Aid loyalty card.

So to the wedding: a grand day; not too hot, not cold and raining. The service was upbeat and not stuffy (the bride and groom high-fived each other when the ceremony was over) and the reception was good fun.

Really, without launching into a story that will take up the next five pages, that's the best I can do; besides, this is their story; the only thing I will say about it is he married up, so we're real proud of him.

Whinge, Britannia

Ah, the British; the people who stood tall against the Hun in two world wars, who stoically withstood The Blitz and who gave us a system of fair and just laws that still form the basis of our legal institutions. So when did they become these cringing little whiners who can't deal with the slightest annoyance?

First, our local Candy Man felt the wrath of the whingers because he had a sense of humor, and now a part-time chicken farmer in Hampshire is in the dock because he has the bad luck to own a rooster that—get this—crows in the morning.

The Candy Man is the affable proprietor of The Candy Box, one of the few remaining independent businesses in Horsham (and Britain, come to that). As he is in possession of a sense of humor, he is in the habit of putting joke headlines on the A-board in front of this shop such as "Swan Sculpture in Suicide Drama," or "Local Youth Kidnapped by Aliens." I really enjoyed those headlines, and used to look forward to seeing them on our evening walks. Not everyone, as it transpired, was amused as I, and whoever it was that managed to take offence, did what any reasonable person, faced with a joke they didn't like, would do: he complained to The Council.

The Council sent the police to persuade The Candy Man to remove the signs and arrest him if he did not. To their consternation, he decided he would rather be arrested. Confused, the police retreated to regroup.

The local press got wind of the incident, then the national press, and when the police returned, determined to take him into custody, they found themselves on the national news. Confused, they retreated to regroup.

The farmer did not fare as well, even though the press also rallied to his defense. His rooster, Rocky, had a penchant for getting up at the crack of dawn (and in the summer, dawn cracks pretty early in these parts) to exercise his vocal chords. His neighbors, on the contrary, liked to sleep in. So they complained to The Council and Rocky was handed a death sentence. Poor Rocky; I at least hope they made a nice Sunday roast with him.

What has gotten into these people? When did they start to feel the need to bother to The Council—while they are trying to deal with stretched budgets, housing shortages and that big pothole on East Street—with such trivialities? And what are these meetings like?

"Oh, oh, Mr. Councilor, that bad Candy Man has put up a sign and it's annoying me!" followed by, "Oh, oh, Mr. Councilor, that bad farmer has a rooster, and it crows in the morning!"

Actually, I don't blame the whingers; no matter where you are you're going to find some cranky nutter who'll complain about anything (hey, what's everyone looking at me for?). No, I blame The Council.

Instead of slapping these people upside the head and telling them to get a life, they say, "Don't you worry, Mr. Whinger, we'll have him arrested." Have the people in charge become so lazy and so unimaginative that the only remedy they can come up with is incarceration? That's something you'd expect from Americans.

As it turns out, our intrepid Candy Man is still entertaining us with his humorous signs, but only because he was willing to accept a criminal record, which left The Council the option of backing off or looking like a right pillock. The farmer, sadly, was not in that position and was forced to send Rocky to the big hen house in the sky. (By the by, they didn't eat him: "Rocky was too old and too tough," the farmer told reporters. "He would have needed to be boiled for several days.")

Conspicuous by their absence in both these cases are the people who complained. Small wonder; how could anyone stand in front of their friends and neighbors and make a case for such a grievance? A rooster crowing? At dawn? In the countryside? Who ever heard of such a thing? As the farmer speculated, "What will be next? Moaning about moo-ing cows and baa-ing sheep?" If these same people lived in a city, would they complain about the sirens at three AM? (Don't laugh, I expect they would.)

But whoever these chronic complainers are, I'm sure they are happy to know that the rooster has been killed and their life can go on in peaceful, unperturbed bliss. At least until the next annoyance sends them running back to The Council:

"Oh, oh, Mr. Council, the bad man—"

"Don't worry, we'll have him arrested."

"But I didn't tell you what he did?"

"Does it matter?"

"Golly, you're the best Council ever; I'll be sure to vote for you next time!"

Oh, have I accidentally hit upon an underlying reason for all this nonsense? Or is it that, in these lean times, cases such as this are regarded as money pumps. After all, the farmer—in addition to being arrested—was fined £5,000 up front and a further £500 a day after that until a final solution was achieved. That's not chicken feed. But the clincher is, the fifty widowed hens are now, reportedly, upset and not laying many eggs, meaning the famer will have to get another rooster or go out of business, even though the manager of The Council's environmental protection team ominously noted of the "Noise Abatement Order" served on the farmer, "It states that he must not have any more noisy cockerels, otherwise they, too, will be covered by the noise abatement notice."

In other words, any time a cock crows on that farm in the future, The Council gets £500.

Cock-(ca-CHING) a doodle doo.

The Hitching Reflex

This is going to make me sound like a grumpy old man (which is a bit unfair because I'm not that old) but I've got to get this off my chest: Now, I know our parents despaired of us and our strange ways, and I despaired of my children, as well, but the current fashion the young people have of wearing their trousers down around their crotches is really driving me crazy.

Dressing like a punk, as my son did, or wearing your jeans until they could stand up on their own, as my friends and I did, was not as irksome as watching young men slouching about with their underwear exposed. I realize teenagers needs to express their individuality by dressing the same as all their friends, but this fashion, as well as being unsightly, looks terribly inconvenient. Why, just for the sake of fitting in, do all these young people put themselves through such ignominy? Even during their busy schedule of hanging around by the fountain, or hanging around outside McDonald's, or hanging around the Subway shop, you'd think one of them might pipe up during a lull in the activity to say, "You know, this way we're dressing, it's really uncomfortable."

The only good thing about it is, you know if one of them mugs you, you're not going to have to chase them very far to get your wallet back. I used to joke about this but I have actually seen it on *Cops Without Guns,* where a young miscreant tried to outrun the police and was captured because his sagging trousers ended up around his ankles.

This fashion, which doesn't appear to be abating, has given rise to what I call "The Hitching Reflex" where young men walk along, taking about five steps, then reflexively grab their trousers and hike them up, only to have them slip down to their thighs after another five steps. Of course you could say, since none of this directly affects me, that I shouldn't be so concerned about it. But what if I want to move someday? How am I supposed to hire some young kid to help me carry a sofa down stairs? He'd either have to carry it one-handed or put it down every fifth step. Either way, I wouldn't be getting my money's worth, even if I only paid him minimum wage.

This "Hitching Reflex" also effects the young ladies, but for a different reason. For those of the fairer sex who do not subscribe to the "loose jeans" theory of fashion and who, instead, complete to see how small a piece of fabric they can wrap around their waist without being arrested for public indecency, an opposite reflex comes into play, causing them to tug at the hem of their belts, I mean, skirts, in an attempt to get the maximum coverage out of the modest amount of cloth they are wearing. (HINT: If you're embarrassed to be seen in public with the bottoms of your knickers showing, wear a longer skirt.)

These similar reflexes give rise to the interesting juxtaposition of seeing a young man shuffling along, treading on the frayed and muddy cuffs of his sagging jeans, hair unkempt and wearing a dirty tee shirt, accompanied by a fetching young woman dressed quiet smartly (though a bit like a tart) in an LBD and new shoes, each of them groping at their own crotches and tugging every few steps.

When I see this, I have to ask, "Why?" Lucky for you, I also have the answer: it's the girl's fault.

C'mon guys, stop thinking about sex long enough to tell me what it is that makes men do the stupid things they do. Oh yeah, sex. Men never do anything unless it is to please a woman. So if these stylish young women—who wish they could wear longer skirts and had boyfriends who at least made an effort to brush their hair and pull up their trousers—put their collective foot down, believe me, the boys would come around right quick.

So gals, do us (and yourselves) all a favor and raise your standards; you'll make this world a better, and more attractive, place to live, and we'll all thank you for it.

Medicine, American Style

No, this isn't going to be a discussion about the current National Health System debate going on in the US. That is way too complicated for me to comment intelligently on and, frankly, I'm not sure how I feel about it myself.

Capitalism can be undeniably ugly, but even the most rapacious robber baron understands you need to keep your customers alive in order to feed your greed. Governments, as history teaches us time and time again, are all too eager to kill the geese to get at the golden eggs inside.

Just my opinion.

But you're not here to study up on National Health Systems; you want to know about my personal health status because, as we know, it's all about me.

Since arriving home from the US, I've been abnormally tired. I chalked it up to jet lag and travel fatigue and waited patiently for my usual pep and impatience to return. A month later, I was still waiting.

By now, I was starting to become concerned. I'm trying hard not to become a hypochondriac, but the Internet makes it difficult. In idle moments, especially when you are not feeling in top shape, it is too tempting to resist entering your symptoms into a search engine and mine the unlimited resources of cyberspace for the host of undesirable diseases that might, at this very moment be lurking inside you waiting their opportunity to strike. So, after a few weeks, I grew tired of scaring myself to death and went to see a real doctor.

To his credit, for being an overworked, underpaid civil servant, he did a thorough job—blood work, ECG, the works—before pronouncing me perfectly healthy and sending me away without any drugs.

What sort of medicine is that? I'm an American, dammit, I want coddling, I want to be assigned a cool-sounding syndrome (Chronic Fatigue Immune Dysfunction Syndrome has a nice ring), I want to be given a note excusing me from pretty much anything I don't want to do for the next three or four months. But here, not even a Lithium tablet; he just said he couldn't believe I had been doing so much in the first place, but without, I might add, advising me to slow down or otherwise allowing me some guilt-free slacker time.

So now there's nothing I can do now except drag my lazy ass back to work.

This is what socialized medicine gets you; I mean, sure he's upset that he's not getting kick-backs from the drug companies like his American counterparts (which explains his reluctance to prescribe any) but you'd think he could have at least recommended a good therapist.

Wanted In America

Ever since The Patriot Act, it's standard practice to have problems getting into America, but this time we're having a problem getting out.

Because my wife is a non-American (i.e. suspected terrorist) she has to follow a more complex protocol when entering and leaving the Land of the Free. Part of this involves a green bit of paper stapled to a page in her passport. This, apparently, is her ticket to Fun Park, USA and, without it, all she can do is look through the fence at the other families having a good time inside. Needless to say, we always make sure she has one.

In the past, this green ticket magically disappeared at one of the check points along our return route, but this time it was still there when we got home. I would have just chucked it away but my wife, not fully trusting the Americans, decided to write to the US Embassy in London about it. Good thing.

The Embassy wrote back a week or so ago. The letter—a masterpiece of soulless, bureaucratic doublespeak, totally devoid of humanity—informed her that, yes, the US Government fully expected that green ticket back. After intimating that it was her fault for not making the customs police do their job correctly, they informed her that, since no one had taken the ticket, she is, as far as the US Government is concerned, still residing in the US. Furthermore, her 6-week visa had expired, so she was not only still in the US, she was in the US illegally.

I'm sure they have the choppers and the K-9 Units out looking for her as we speak.

She was instructed to send the green ticket to the US Embassy in London, Kentucky (and I'm sure the irony was wasted on them) immediately along with proof that she was, indeed, back in England.

This had us stumped. A copy of receipts for airline tickets would only prove we had receipts for airline tickets, not that we were on the plane. The same with itineraries or pretty much anything else we could think of. I offered to take a photo of her standing outside our apartment building holding a copy of today's *Daily Mail* but she said she doubted they would accept that and, besides, she wouldn't be caught dead holding a copy of the *Daily Mail*.

Ominously, she was advised to check her status in a few weeks time to see if the bureaucrats in London, Kentucky were any better than the bureaucrats who failed to take the green ticket in the first place. If the green ticket did not successfully complete its odyssey, and the proper paperwork was not filed, they would continue to assume she was living in the US illegally and could deny her entry next time she came to visit. (You would think showing up at the border would be a sure-fire method of proving you were no longer in the country, but apparently not to these guys.)

To check her status, she needs to "file a Freedom…" And there our bureaucratic friends let us down. The following page was missing, leaving us to wonder what, exactly, we need to file. A Freedom Maxipad tally for the past seven years, in duplicate? A Freedom Trail Hiking Certificate dated no later than 1987? A Freedom Isn't Free essay, 3,000 words, double-spaced on 8 ½ x 11 20 lb bond white paper (none of this commie A4 nonsense, thank you very much)?

So now we have letters going all over: back to London (England) to ask for page two of their communication so we can figure out what to file, over to London (Kentucky) to attempt to prove my wife is not living as an illegal alien somewhere in mid-state New York, and, once we know what to file and where to file it, we'll need to send a request for my wife's updated alien status and agreement that they will allow her back in should the need arise.

I suppose we shouldn't sweat it; the worst case scenario would simply involve my wife spending a few days on her own in Canada while I popped down to visit the family. Maybe I could even convince them all to come up to Rouses Point so they could stand on the US side of the bridge and wave to my wife on the other side. In the long run, that would probably be simpler.

My Day Job

I work with computers, and while I make it a point to not talk about my office life, I feel it is my duty to try to illustrate to you non-computer people what working with computers is like; it may keep you from making a serious career move error.

To keep it simple, let's equate any of the myriad of simple tasks I have to perform during the course of my work day to something that you can readily relate to: your task is to come home, hang your coat on the hook in the hallway and eat dinner before going out with your friends to the pub. That's it; a sequence of two simple tasks followed by a reward.

So you enter your home and hang your coat on the hook.

It falls on the floor.

You pick the coat up and check it. There is nothing wrong with it. You hang it on the hook again.

It falls on the floor.

You check the hook; there is nothing wrong with it. You hang your coat on the hook again.

It falls on the floor.

You try to hang your coat on the second hook, instead.

It falls on the floor.

You take a scarf off of the third hook and hang it on the second hook.

It stays in place.

You hang your jacket on the second hook.

It falls on the floor.

You hang the scarf on the first hook.

It falls on the floor.

You put the scarf back where you got it on the third hook.

It falls on the floor.

You now methodically try hanging your jacket and the scarf on each of the three hooks and watch as they each fall to the floor every time.

You mumble to yourself for a while, then do a Google search on the specific style, brand and version of the hooks.

You find there is a "known Issue" with this type of hook which causes anything hung on the first hook to be ever after unusable on any hook.

After an hour of perusing help forums and technical blogs, you resign yourself to the fact that there is nothing you can do about this. You are advised not to try, under any circumstances, removing the hooks and replacing them in a different order because it won't help.

You remove the hooks and replace them in a different order.

It doesn't help.

You remove the hooks, throw them away and go to the nearest hardware store.

It's closed.

You go to the next one.

It's closed.

You find an open one in an industrial estate 20 miles away. The man says you should have kept the hooks; he knows a way they can be fixed.

You buy three different hooks and return home.

The new hooks are not compatible with the base board the original hooks were installed on.

You return to the hardware store and buy a multi-functional baseboard.

The new baseboard needs modification before it can be affixed to the wall. This causes the hooks, which now fit, to be fastened upside down. They work fine, but you still can't hang anything on any of them.

You pick up your coat and scarf, fold them up and put them in the linen cupboard.

You try, but fail, to convince yourself that this is a better solution than the hooks anyway.

By now your friends are having a great time at the pub and you have not actually completed your first task. Still, you might just be able to make last call if you cook and eat your dinner quickly.

You head to the kitchen, take a ready-meal out of the fridge and put it in the oven.

The oven won't light.

Train Besotted

I am not a trainspotter—one of the bevy of men and boys who cluster at the ends of the platforms with notebooks, cameras and packed lunches—but I seem to be unable to resist the urge to take a photo of every railroad station I stop at. And not just the ones I have never visited before; I take a photo of every station every time I'm there.

I can't help it; I find train travel romantic. Admittedly, train riding here isn't quite the same as riding through the night in a boxcar making the long and lonely ramble across the American prairie, but I was never able to do that (the guards caught us and sent us home to our moms), so I have to settle for the remnants of British Rail. Still, nothing offers such hope, inspires such despair, weighs you down with such dark desolation or lifts your spirits with such heady promise as a train station.

The joy of arriving at a desirable destination and the ache of leaving one (or the joy of leaving Haywards Heath at 11:14 PM) is as unmatchable as the purposeful bustle of a busy terminal or the quiet contemplativeness of a deserted platform. If you are heading out on a long journey, you can stow your luggage, take off your jacket and settle down with the beer you bought from the bubbly blonde with the Slavic cheek bones and unintelligible accent pushing the beverage cart, or, if you choose, you can nap to the subtle sway (or violent lurching) of the carriage. On a short, commuter run, you can jam in with your fellow commuters and, even on the most depressing of mornings, feel at one with humanity and take succor from the fact that you are not the skinny young man wedged between the two curvaceous council estate queens, one of whom is applying rouge with a paint brush while the other is shouting into her mobile phone—in graphic detail—about her adventures of the previous night that, unless you overheard wrong, involved a Panamanian midget and a golden retriever.

But I digress.

Who but the most jaded of travelers would not find himself gazing about in country-boy wonder when first arriving at St. Pancras station? How could you fail to be inspired by the technological and aesthetic achievement of the coastline run between Totnes and Taunton? And where else could you get a palpable sense of having been transported back in time except by stepping from a train onto the platform at Torfaen in Wales?

And nothing on this earth can conjure up such simultaneously lugubrious and wistfully idealistic imagery as sipping a cup of coffee in an old-fashioned cafe at an isolated station in the rain. I'm there now, at the Whistle Stop Cafe in Totnes, staring out the windows as the trains chug through the driving rain and it's hard to imagine a setting which could inspire a more reflectively pensive mood than I am in right now.

It's a sweet feeling; nostalgic, aching, lonely and buoyant all at the same time. The juxtapositions abound—the wet chill outside verses the warm comfort of coffee, the cacophony of the trains versus quiet contemplation, the loneliness that clings like stale cigarette smoke to the scarred plastic table covers, dusty windows and well-trodden door mat versus the homecoming that is now merely hours away.

A freight train is rumbling past. I don't see very many of them in Britain, but when I do they never fail to remind me of the States. Back there, they were so long that, when we had to stop at a crossing to let one go by, people would get out of their cars and watch. Together we would stand with the other families on the dirt road, counting the boxcars until we lost track. They would roll by so slowly you could run and catch up with one, jumping on board to ride the rails with the hobos and men of the road. But you wouldn't; you'd stand with your parents, watching the impossibly long train disappear into the distance like a ghost.

This one didn't take so long to pass; it only had eight cars, hardly enough to make me thoughtful, let alone melancholy. Time to finish my coffee and step out into the rain. My train will be here soon, and I want to get a picture of the station before it's too late.

"Take Me to the American Embassy"

That's what I said as I jumped into the cab outside of Victoria Station.

"I've always wanted to say that," I told the driver as I settled in. He looked at me in the mirror; his expression never wavered.

"The Embassy, Sir?"

Some people just have no appreciation for the dramatic.

For the record, I hate going to the American Embassy, but when you need something notarized, that's where you have to go: twenty quid for the train ride, six quid for the cab fare and thirty dollars for the service (not to mention the wasted vacation day), all for something that, in the States, you can get Cindy in accounting to do for free during your coffee break.

Moreover, I hate the look of the embassy, with all its razor wire, men with machine guns and concrete blockades. It looks like a besieged city block in downtown Baghdad, not the outpost of a free, strong and confident nation; though, I must admit they've made some improvements since my last visit and it is much more aesthetically pleasing now. There is no double boundary of concrete and razor wire, just the normal, wrought iron fence, a temporary and unobtrusive wire fence inside that, and a fetching granite skirt around the base of the building that takes the place of the unsightly concrete barriers. And the ubiquitous, smartly dressed men brandishing machine guns.

Also changed was the manner of entry. It used to be that you showed up at the gate, stated your business and were admitted. Now there are two out buildings with a line for each. I asked a guard what to do and he pointed me toward one of the lines. After a while, another guard asked to see my passport, state my business and told me I couldn't go inside with my suitcase. (Just so you know; I had the suitcase with me because I was heading out on a business trip, not planning to seek asylum).

The woman told me I had to check my luggage. She pointed to a large white truck down the street and told me that was where I needed to go.

When I got to the truck, imagining it to be some sort of bomb-proof holding tank, I discovered it was, in fact, a garbage truck. I didn't credit the Americans with that level of taking the piss, so I returned to the embassy and asked another guard what to do.

"Go ask the man standing by the buildings," he told me.

"I did ask him," I said. "He sent me to that line, and the guard at that line sent me to that garbage truck."

I was eventually made to understand that it wasn't the truck I was to go to, but the pharmacy the truck was parked in front of.

The pharmacy was run by a Pakistani gentleman who didn't seem to mind absorbing a possible hit on the embassy. He charged four pounds a bag and provided advice for free.

"You must leave everyting here," he said in broken English. "Laptop, camera, phone, USB sticks, iPod, everyting. You would be surprised what they don't let in. Some people come back tree, four times. They let you wear your trouser, but everyting else you must leave here."

Let me tell you, you never appreciate how many electronic doodads you are dependent upon until you visit the American Embassy.

Back in line, and safely away from any bombs that might be behind the counter at the pharmacy, I realized I still had two USB sticks in my briefcase and a (gulp) Swiss Army penknife in my pocket. When my turn at the security bunker came, I tossed my tiny knife into the bin with the rest of my pocket paraphernalia and covered it all with my jacket in the hope that they might miss it. Fat chance.

To their credit, they didn't shout, "KNIFE!" pull their weapons and draw down on me while screaming, "ON THE FLOOR, SCUMBAG!" They just put it in a plastic bag along with the two USB sticks and made me leave it at the desk.

The remainder of the visit went smoothly enough and the clerks were even mildly polite. (I've always suspected the embassy staff resent us expats. After all, they're loyal American citizens simply posted temporarily abroad while they do their bit for the government; we're lousy turncoats who chose to move away from the greatest country in the world.)

I have no doubt that the whole process is carefully orchestrated to confound and intimidate. It's their first line of defense:

"Achmed, where do we go to put the bomb? That woman told me to stand in this line here."

"I don't know, Jabar. That guard told me to stand in the line over there."

"This is very confusing, and they all look terribly cross."

"I know a good restaurant on Bond Street; let's go for a Balti curry, instead."

"But the bomb, what do we do with it?"

"That man with the machine gun said we should leave it with the pharmacist down the street."

A Tale of Two Thanksgivings

1968

I'm 13, and there's no school, so I'm up early. Not as early as my mom; no one ever gets up as early as my mom, but today she is up extra early, singing in the kitchen, rattling pots and pans. She isn't preparing a turkey—we have Thanksgiving dinner at my grandma's house—but she is making pancakes for breakfast, pumpkin pies to bring to the dinner and sugar cookies for later.

Soon the whole family is up. We have a big breakfast together, which is, in itself, unusual. At ten o'clock, it's time for the first tradition: gathering the ground pine for the Christmas wreath.

I take two brown paper bags and my little brother, Marc. He's nine now and old enough to be useful though still too young to be very interesting. We walk down the dirt lane and then cut into the woods. There is no snow yet, but the fields are frosty and the puddles in the marshy ground are thick with ice. We amuse each other by smashing them; as much fun as breaking windows and with no undesirable side-effects.

I know where to hunt for the ground pine and sweep away the frosted leaves with a gloved hand to reveal the little tree-like evergreen shoots. Together we pull up long strands, stuffing the bags full.

At home, my sister is on the phone with her boyfriend and the Macy's Day parade is on the TV. We watch it while wrapping the ground pine around a bent coat hanger, adding layer after layer while the big, balloons float by on the TV screen. By the time the finale arrives—Santa in his sleigh heralding the official start of the Christmas season—the wreath is done. My mother makes it more festive with some red ribbon and aerosol snow and hangs it on the front door.

Then we leave for grandma's, the five of us kids stuffed into the backseat singing, "Over the river and through the woods, to grandmother's house we go!" After a while my mom joins in. My dad stays silent.

Grandma's kitchen is warm and redolent with the smell of turkey and fresh baked biscuits. My uncles are there, with their wives and children and various boyfriends. We horse around in the chicken coop and play hide and seek among the farm machinery until dinner is ready.

This is a special year, I'm promoted to the grown up table with my older sister, Melinda, while Marc, Matt and Michelle have to sit with their young cousins at the kiddie table. Then the feast appears: stuffing, hot and moist, yams, mashed potatoes, gravy, green beans with slivers of almond, creamed corn, boiled carrots, cranberry sauce out of a can, biscuits and, as the main event, turkey, golden brown and steaming as my grandfather cuts into it.

After we've eaten so much we think we can't take another bite, out come the pumpkin pies, mincemeat pies, ice cream, whipped cream and that strange concoction made out of marshmallows, Cool Whip, Jell-o and slivers of tangerine that I never see at any other time of the year but always look forward to.

And after the feast there is a long, languid afternoon that turns into evening with an impromptu dinner of, what else, turkey and stuffing and gravy and…

Much later, on the verge of sleep, my aunts, uncles and grandparents draw a reluctant end to their jovial conversations and we all trundle into the car and back home.

It's late, and I'm stuffed but there is still time, and just enough room, to sample one of my mom's sugar cookies.

2010

I'm (you do the math) and my cell phone, which doubles as a travel alarm clock, buzzes me awake. I'm on yet another business trip and I wander around the tiny hotel room, checking my e-mails between showering and getting ready for the day. I have toast for breakfast and head to the client's offices. It's another long and grueling session; we don't break for lunch.

Back at the hotel, I have the steak and kidney pie for dinner because there is nothing on the menu that remotely resembles turkey. No one remarks that it is Thanksgiving; no one knows.

After dinner, I sit outside in the crisp night, watching the cars and the people go by, smoking a cigar and drinking a pint of ale. It's a lonely business, traveling for work. But it's not a bad sort of loneliness because I know it will soon be over and I will return home to my wife.

This isn't where I thought I would be those many years ago, sitting by myself in a strange town thousands of miles from where I was born. I miss the holiday, and I miss gathering with friends and family on this day that is special only to Americans. But we go where life takes us, and even though I did not have a dinner of turkey, stuffing and cranberry sauce, I'm still grateful. When you take away the feast and the fellowship, that's what Thanksgiving is really all about, counting your blessings, and remembering that you have much to be thankful for.

And so, here on my own, I count them; they are many, and I am thankful for each and every one.

The Technicolor Yawn

opefully, you won't think this represents a new low for me, but while I was up last night talking to Ralph on the Big White Phone, it occurred to me that we haven't really broached that subject, and now is the perfect time for it. If you're a bit squeamish, or would like to continue to think of this book as a welcome oasis of quality writing, you might be better off skipping to the next chapter.

Giving your meal a round-trip ticket is no joy in any circumstance, but this particular episode took place while we were staying with friends. We'd spent a lovely afternoon browsing around Arundel, a quaint little town with a castle and a cathedral that, as a bonus, happened to be having it's Christmas Fete while we were there. There were bands and beer booths and the type of small town festivities you generally only see in *Midsomer Murders*. Afterward, we retired to our friends' manor for dinner and some postprandial libations. We had a nice chat, then retired.

An hour later my eyes shot open and I found myself fully awake in an unfamiliar room wondering what it was that roused me. And a voice, way in the back of my mind whispered:

"Get ready, you're going to throw up."

"Hey, who said that? That's a perfectly ludicrous idea. Get it out of your head right now. Think good thoughts. Yes, that's better."

"No, I think you're about to toss your cookies."

"Clearly not! Stop thinking that!"

"Sorry, but it's true."

This went on for some time. I don't know about you, but this is necessary for me, it is a sort of coming to terms, my "seven stages" of nausea, if you will. It suits me well because, by the time I reach acceptance and head for the porcelain bus, I am immediately ready to start driving, so to speak. And that's a good thing, because once you assume the position, there's no sense in hanging about.

And so I stumbled through the darkness, found the little room and proceeded to serve up what looked like a Dulux color chart.

Over the years, having been in a variety of relationships, I have had occasion to be around other people while they were making friends with the toilet and I have always marveled at the ones—and this means almost all of them—who manage this feat in relative silence. I once had the opportunity to witness the young lady in the seat next to me making use of her air-sickness bag, and if I hadn't known what the bag was for, I would have had no idea what she was doing. (I have always dreaded having to make use of one. Have you seen the size of them? I could fill three with the first gastro geyser. I'd have to have a line of people on one side passing them to me and another line to pass the full ones to.)

Anyway, you get my point, many people seem to be able to have dinner in reverse gear in relative silence—I, however, cannot. When I start calling the buffalos, that's exactly what it sounds like; this is an activity I like to share with the rest of the household, the neighbors, and the people down the street.

Chagrined as I was, I put it down to excess and returned to bed. An hour later I was wide awake and arguing with myself once more, signifying that it wasn't a drink-induced spewing, but a bona fide illness. This continued on an hourly basis until I had fully reviewed the day's menu. My friend, who drank as much whiskey as I had, slept blissfully through it, but his wife, with her mother-radar, was not so fortunate.

In the morning, I felt like ten miles of bad road, but my wife and I managed to make our way home without incident (read: I didn't make a carpet pizza on the train) and I slept the day away.

I feel marginally better now (thanks for asking) but, with another three day business trip beginning tomorrow at 5 AM, I find myself wavering as to my fitness for such a task. Part of me wants to just stay in bed for the next few days, but the other part of me (that tiny portion some people call "responsibility" but I refer to as "that sanctimonious prig") insists that is not an option.

I suppose the only thing I can do is pack, get ready, and see if I can go the night without yodeling down the porcelain canyon.

The Wild West

The saloonkeeper looked up from wiping the bar when the mysterious stranger entered. He dried his hands on his soiled apron and waited wordlessly while the stranger approached.

"Coffee," said the stranger, with the rough voice of a man who has been long on the trail.

"Sure thing, pardner."

"And breakfast; full English."

The stranger tossed a coin onto the bar.

"Keep the change."

The saloon was empty, and looked as if it had been for some time. The smell of dim despair tinged with resignation and the sweat of weary travelers permeated the room. The stranger found a seat at a table in the corner. Outside, the rain beat a languid, lonely rhythm.

(Okay, so I'm not a mysterious stranger in a bad western, but cut me a break; it's 6:22 on Wednesday morning, I've been on the road since Sunday, it's raining and Totnes is deserted. The hotel promised to serve me breakfast even though I told them I was leaving ungodly early, but when I came down this morning I could find no one—that's no one—in the entire building. So I'm back at the Signal Box Cafe at Totnes station, waiting for a train.)

The saloonkeeper served up the meal and the stranger ate the surprisingly bland eggs in silence (how can they make eggs this bland—an egg is an egg for chrissake!). Then Gabbie, the old prospector—who has been too long up in the mountains with only ol' Sal, his mule, for company—pushed through the swinging door.

"Cold out there! Cold and wet! I need me some tea. You got tea? How much is it?"

The saloonkeeper watched him through hooded eyes.

"Seventy-five pence."

Gabbie dropped his prospecting sack and sat heavily at a nearby table.

"Good. That's good. I'll have tea. Thank you, sir! My, that's a fine cup of tea, yes sir."

Gabbie spied the rack of promotional brochures.

"Say, you don't mind if I have a few of those? Oh, The Eden Project. I've been there! And Bunting Hole Railway, and the Not-Quite-Land's-End Theme Park. And where is The Rogered Sheep Inn? Is that in Cumbria or the Isle of Man?"

He seemed to be addressing an invisible companion standing very close to him. When the invisible companion didn't answer, Gabbie continued his soliloquy.

"Not headin' there today, mind, no sir, no sir, I'm for Plymouth, soon as I make them give me my money back. Oh, they took it off me, right as rain, they did. I'll get it back. You bet I will."

The saloonkeeper's wife scurried out the side door. The mysterious stranger watched in silence.

(Actually, it wasn't really Gabbie the old prospector, I think it was some local nutter who escaped from the home. And the saloonkeeper's wife—sorry, the cafe manger's wife—didn't go to fetch the cops as I had thought. She was probably just nipping down to Morrisons to pick up some milk, so I can't have the local sheriff—in the guise of PCSO Dobson—bursting into the saloon. Pity, that.)

Meanwhile, back in the saloon, Gabbie is still rifling through the brochures and talking to people who aren't there.

"You don't mind me takin' these? Don't need those there; I been there, but these here, I want to go someday. Soon as I get my money, you bet I will, they took it from me, you know, and I told them when they took it, I told them I would—"

"THE TRAIN NOW APPROCHING PLATFORM TWO IS THE 6:50 TO EDINBURGH, CALLING AT NEWTON-ABBOTT, EXETER SAINT DAVID'S—"

"No! No! I don't want Exeter, I want Plymouth! Not going to Exeter, not at all. Stop! Stop!"

(Ah, arguing with the voices; I'm with you, mate.)

"Change at Taunton," the saloonkeeper said, as the locomotive, belching smoke and sparks from the massive, coal-fired engine, squealed and hissed to a shuddering halt.

"Board!" shouted the porter from the platform outside.

Gabbie stuffed the brochures in his sack. The mysterious stranger picked up his saddlebags and headed toward the door.

"If I miss this train, when's the next one? How many are there?" Gabbie's plaintive eyes sought out the mysterious stranger. "How am I going to get to Torquay?"

The stranger looked at Gabbie.

"I don't know, pardner," he said, stepping into the dark, morning rain. "I'm just passing through."

(And the coolest thing about this story is, that is actually what I said.)

Jumper Weather

It's cold here, and has been for some time. About mid-December the temperature dropped below freezing and it's just kept going down ever since. Lately, the days are routinely in the high teens or low twenties, residing in a temperature zone I like to call "New York Cold."

This is not necessarily a bad thing, as it gives the locals a chance to complain about the weather (and the British are never happier than when they are complaining about the weather) and it means I have the chance to wear my jumpers. (For you Americans who have not seen *Bridget Jones' Diary*, let me assure you that I am not parading about wearing the type of dress the British refer to as a Pinafore; what I am referring to are sweaters.) When I lived in the States, winter was all about jumpers. There's nothing like sitting snug on the sofa wearing a comfy old sweater, but here, even though, in the past, I enthusiastically pulled on a jumper to ward off the morning chill, I had to remove it by noon because I was sweating.

Not this year. Over the past weeks I have gone through the few old favorites I brought with me from the States, and even had to go to the Edinburgh Woollen Mill on West Street to pick up a few more in the Christmas Sales. Now I have about six, which should see me through to spring, a big change from New York, where I measured my sweaters in feet. They occupied a place of honor on my closet shelf, one stacked upon the other, and each one told its own story.

There was a time, during one of my protracted periods of bachelorhood, when every woman who knew me for more than two consecutive weeks would buy me a sweater as a sort of territorial marker, similar to the way dogs urinate on fire hydrants. Since sweater season runs from about the end of August through to May, there was a good chance that anyone who made it past the second date would show up on the third with a sweater and expect me to wear it.

Not that I minded; it was a ritual as familiar and comforting as the jumpers themselves, and after a time, they began to serve as a woolen history, enabling me to read through my past relationships by looking at the pile of sweaters in the same way a geologist can read the eras of the earth's history in the layers of rock on a cliff face.

So bring on the cold (but, really, let's not get carried away with it); as long as I have jumpers and hot cocoa, I'll be a happy man.

The Siege—Day 22

On the 17th of December, the temperature dropped below freezing. On the 18th, it snowed. The snow and the cold are still here, and so are we, living in our sitting room as if it is the Castle Keep, venturing into the frigid "East Wing" of the flat only to forage for food or visit the loo.

On the first day of the siege, the sitting room heater broke (again) and we had to move the bedroom heater into The Keep. This was when we discovered that, no matter how many blankets you pile on the bed, sleeping in sub-freezing temperatures is no picnic.

On the second day I called Cynthia to tell her about the broken heater.

On the third day, I got through to Cynthia and she promised to tell the contractor.

On the fourth day, the contractor checked the heater, refused to believe it was broken and declined to replace it.

On the fifth day, I went out and bought my own heater (again). This allowed us to reclaim the bedroom and make it an annex to The Keep.

The Holiday Season provided some welcome diversion, not to mention provisions, but by New Year we were already running low on mince pies.

Later that week, we found ourselves low on milk, and in order to conserve milk for our tea, we start drinking wine.

The next day we ran out of pancake mix, Coffee Mate and Bisto Gravy Granules.

A few days later, we found ourselves running alarmingly low on wine. To help out, I began drinking whiskey. (You don't think the worst spell of weather to hit Britain in the last 30 years has stopped me from partaking in my "beverage and cigar on the balcony" ritual, do you?)

On day twenty-one, after spending two full days in the flat, I popped out for ten minutes to mail a letter. During that time, Parcel Force visited, leaving a note chiding me for not being in when they tried to deliver a package.

Today, day twenty-two of The Siege, I trekked into town to buy a half-gallon of milk.

I knew I was in for it when there were only two shopping trolleys in the cart corral. Inside the store, it looked as if people were preparing for Armageddon. The shelves were all but picked bare. There was no semi-skimmed milk available, only full fat. And of that, there was only one (yes, one) gallon jug of milk and the lady in front of me snapped it up before I could get to it. All that remained were liter jugs, so I picked one of those up and elbowed my way through the store to join a queue for a till that stretched halfway down the bakery aisle.

Everyone around me had carts piled high with apocalyptic panic purchases: goat's milk, blueberry muffin mix, gallon jugs of extra virgin olive oil, cans of corned beef, parsnips, toaster waffles. I felt like an amateur standing there with nothing but a liter of milk and a canister of gravy granules (you can't expect me to get through a siege without gravy, can you?).

So now I'm back in The Keep, drinking tea with full-fat milk—which tastes odd after all these years of enforced semi-skimmed milk drinking—and waiting for more snow. We did find a container of powdered milk that might do in a pinch. It has an expiration date of June 2005, but that stuff doesn't go bad, does it?

The news is the same tonight as it has been for the past three weeks—cold, snow, no end in sight and aren't we rubbish for not being able to cope with it. I never liked this sort of weather when I lived in America and I'm not any more fond of it here. But one thing I did learn during all those long, cold, snowy Upstate winters was this: spring has its own schedule but it will, on some distant and happy day, arrive.

So I'll be fine, as long as the whiskey holds out.

Waiting for Godot

I'm standing on a train platform in Newport, Wales, wondering what is going to arrive first, my connection to Reading, or Whitsun. If it's Whitsun, the holiday schedule will kick in, and I won't be going anywhere; if it's my train, it will be a miracle. It's sort of like watching, *Waiting for Godot*, except that, in the play, Godot is more likely to show up.

This has been an interesting trip, more so than most because I went to a place I have never been to before, and that always opens up opportunities for adventure. In this case, I was heading to a tiny town in Wales somewhere north of Newport and south of Aberystwyth. Seasoned traveler that I am, I had prepared by checking maps, gathering data and collating all the information I could possibly need onto a single piece of paper that I tucked into my shirt pocket.

My preparation seemed flawless until the train stopped and I stepped out into the middle of nowhere. Literally. It was a slab of concrete surrounded by forest and struck me as the kind of place where, if they had a bombing, no one would notice.

The car park was empty, there was no taxi rank and the exit lane from the lot joined a dual-highway that didn't invite foot traffic, so I went back to the platform and called the only cab company listed on the bulletin board.

"Can't help you, mate," said the man who answered the phone. "Car's gone in for a brake job." Then he hung up. I pulled out my treasure trove of information only to discover there was nothing of any use on it. I had thought to record the address of the hotel, but not the phone number.

Undeterred, I recalled the hotel had sent me a "Thanks for booking us and not Travel Lodge" text, so I scrolled through my call register until I found it.

"Sure, we can send you a cab," Cindy Howcanihelpyou told me. "But it might be fifteen or twenty minutes."

I assured her I wasn't going anywhere.

The cab arrived and, with the help of the hotel address, brought me to a large roundabout on the dual highway where I spent the night surrounded by a moat of motorized concrete. In the morning I called for another cab. The same guy showed up.

The address for the client was an industrial estate. A big one. And that was as specific as it got. I had the cab drop me off in front of a random building where I discovered my information sheet did not contain the names of the people I was going to meet, the address of the place to meet them or a phone number to call them.

I did know I could get all this data from my laptop so, with my briefcase lying open on the frosty ground, I balanced my laptop on a railing and tried to locate the e-mails and documents containing the absent information. At this time, a woman came out of the building and asked if she could help me.

I didn't bother trying to tell her I had everything under control, I was just glad to get some assistance so I wouldn't look like a berk in front of the people I was coming to meet. The people I was coming to meet, however, turned out to be her and her boss.

I do this for a living, honest.

Despite the bumpy beginning, it was a good visit. At the end of the day I called for a cab and the same guy showed up. Clearly he was the only cab operating in that part of Wales with a functioning vehicle (although from the look of it, it barely passed that requirement), but the driver was affable and helpful and seemed to know the area. He brought me back to the train station, if you could call it that, and warned that the train might not stop if it didn't see anyone on the platform. I knew he wasn't joking as the announcements in the train going up advised passengers for certain stations to notify the conductor if they wanted the train to stop there. So I made myself visible on the platform—not difficult as I was the only fixture.

The train showed up, and it did stop, but it wasn't in any hurry to get anywhere. I worried the entire trip about making my connection, even though I should have known better. I'm at Newport now, and of the four trains due in over the next half hour, three are running late, and the one running the latest is mine.

I wonder if that old guy wrapped in the duffle coat and napping on the bench is Godot.

After All This Time

After all this time in England, I feel I have adapted fairly well to my adopted country. I can travel around without getting lost, I complain about the weather with the best of them, and I even speak the language like a native. But I still cannot get to grips with eggs, electricity, aspirin and time.

The electrical sockets here are 220 volt. Yes, even for a night light or a Glade Room Freshener. This makes the Brits very cautious around electricity and practically eliminates amusing anecdotes about the time you convinced your little brother to stick a bobby pin into an outlet. As a safety precaution, wall plugs have switches on them, so you can turn the power off "at the mains."

This is all well and good, as long as you remember to turn it on at the mains. I wish I had a 5 pence piece for every time my laptop ran out of power or I turned a light on and off half a dozen times wondering what was wrong with it or I returned to the kitchen after 20 minutes to see why I didn't smell dinner cooking only to find the stove stone cold and the mains power still switched off.

And time, over here, is military-style, with trains arriving and leaving at such times as 16:34 or 19:04. And for some reason, I just cannot get used to this. The simple formula of subtracting 2 and losing the first digit (turning 18:46 into 16:46 or 6:46, for example) often has me thinking that my 18:47 train is due at 16:47 so that would make it 4:47. Even with a 24-hour watch, I would still have problems adjusting. The whole thing gives me a headache.

Which brings me to aspirin. The abiding belief in Britain that eating a handful of aspirin is a viable method of topping yourself means you cannot buy it by the gross, as in the US. So I am forced to buy it in boxes of 12. And you can only buy one at a time. Consequently, when I get a headache, I have to go buy a box, take two and then put the box somewhere that I will remember it in the future. The medicine cabinet seems like a good place, and I swear that is where I put them, but weeks later, when I have another headache, the box has disappeared. So I have to buy another box.

Somewhere in this flat, there are about 187 12-packs of aspirin with 10 tablets left in them. I expect we'll find them if we ever move out.

As for eggs, I spent 46 years developing the perfect tapping technique for cracking an American egg and then found out—to my bitter disappointment—that the skill is non-transferable. The problem, in my opinion, is they don't feed their chickens enough DDT or whatever it is we feed them in the States because the shells here (on their brown, not white, eggs) are hard as walnuts.

Since it is my privilege to make breakfast on weekend mornings, and since my vegetarian wife and I have a limited selection of foods in common, a typical morning meal inevitably includes eggs. A favorite of mine is eggs over easy, and my wife likes fried eggs (they are the same thing, by the way) but the odds of me getting a yolk out of an eggshell in one piece are about the same as the Labour government sweeping to victory at the polls in the next general election.

Now, I know from experience that I have to hit the egg harder than I am used to, so I steel myself and give it a good whack. Generally, the first blow glances off the armor plating leaving hardly a nick. The second blow, delivered with more determination, adds a dent and a few cracks. So the third blow is practically guaranteed to end up with me holding a dripping mass of canary yellow goo, splintered eggshell and a good deal of something that unnervingly resembles snot in my hand.

We eat a lot of scrambled eggs.

But only if I remember to turn the stove on at the mains.

The One Where
I Play Cricket

We had our annual office picnic a few weeks back, which in and of itself was not very funny. But at the picnic, a cricket game was organized and, although I determinedly voiced my unsuitableness as a player, I was equally determinedly recruited.

"But I don't even know how to hold a cricket bat," I protested.

"Thin side up," they said. "The rest is easy."

"I won't know what to do."

"You'll catch on; it's sort of like baseball."

"But I was rubbish at baseball!"

The argument that pushed me into willingly joining in was when they said: "Think of the humor potential."

Fortunately, it was a friendly game, involving a mix of children and adults. It was also an unorthodox game, following a complex set of rules (such as, if it lands in the hedge, that's minus 5) and designed to allow maximum participation for all players. Unfortunately, that meant I had to take my turn at pitching and couldn't simply stand in the outer, outside outfield, like I always did when forced to participate in a baseball game.

Although unaccustomed to baseball, I am still an American, and I think there is some sort of race-memory at work where Americans and baseball are concerned because when I was up at bat, I only knew how to bat like an American.

In baseball, when the pitch is thrown and you either swing at it or let it go by and hope the ump shouts, "BALL!" In cricket, although part of the point is to hit the ball, your main objective is to protect an unstable construction of sticks, called a wicket. Hitting the ball is incidental, and running—whether or not you actually hit the ball—is optional.

Imagine my confusion.

But believe it or not, it wasn't swinging, missing, hitting or running that caused me the most problems, it was the habit baseball players have of wandering around between pitches. Unless you hit the ball and run, there is a period of down time before the next pitch and an aimless ramble—which gives you time to spit, take practice swings or knock the dirt out of your cleats—seems the logical, if not traditional, way to fill it. In cricket, I discovered, this leaves your wicket unprotected, providing the ten-year-old kid behind you the opportunity of tossing the ball at the wicket to knock the little horizontal thingies off of the upright sticks.

This happened every time I missed the ball, which, quite frankly, was a lot. No matter how I coached myself, I would always take a little stroll after missing a pitch and the kid would always tag me out.

The other baseball instinct wasn't so much of an instinct as it was just plain common sense. When it was my turn to pitch, I threw the ball the only way I knew how (i.e. the way a normal person would), which my British colleagues thought highly amusing. I found this strange, considering how they pitch.

First of all, they don't pitch; they "bowl." And the bowler doesn't stand on a mound, he runs a great distance (generally from the outer outfield where my preferred fielding position is) before winding up and hurling the ball in a comical overhand arc straight at...the ground. Unlike in baseball, where the pitcher tries to hit the batter in the head, the cricket bowler skillfully bounces the ball so that, as it reaches the batter, it will be at the exact height of his testicles, I mean, the wicket. Actually, they are about one and the same, which I have to suppose was done on purpose to keep the batters on their toes and bring a hint of excitement to a game that is, to be kind, God's own answer to insomnia.

In retrospect, what surprised me most was not how my baseball instincts made me a rubbish cricket player, but how the most inbred of baseball habits—that of throwing the bat after hitting the ball—managed to avoid manifesting itself.

I'm sure some of you Americans are thinking, "So?" but trust me on this; it would have been the wrong thing to do. It's the sort of thing the Brits might consider typical of a vulgar colonial, but would be too polite to mention. Plus it really would have pissed off the kid who owned the bat, though it would serve him right for tagging me out so often.

The Senior Prom

Time was, when you heard a Brit say, "I'm going to the prom," you could safely believe they were heading to Brighton for a walk along the seafront or had just bought tickets for BBC's Classic Music Festival. Now, you have to consider the possibility that they are looking forward to yet another American intrusion into British life—the end of school dance.

This is a relatively recent interloper; just a few years ago the phenomenon was practically unheard of, but recently the idea of a ball-type celebration has wormed its way into the hearts and heads of British teenagers and the wallets of their parents.

The cultural aspects surrounding the phenomenon of a British Senior Prom are baffling.

First and foremost, they do not have Seniors here so they cannot have a Senior Prom. The school systems are different. While in the US, you enter high school at 13 or 14 (that would be the 9th grade, or your Freshman year) and leave at 17 or 18, after your Senior year, the British end school at 15 or 16 and then go to college. But their college isn't like college in the US, which is more like what the Brits call "university."

It's all very confusing, but the bottom line is, Americans look upon the Senior Prom as a sort of ritual ushering them into adulthood, which at 17 or 18 is appropriate. What you have here are a bunch of 15-year-old kids playing dress-up at mummy and daddy's expense. Not that there is anything wrong with that, as long as mummy and daddy have a spare 800 quid lying around, I'm just saying that there is no real correlation between a US Senior Prom and a British end of school year fancy dance.

Now, I didn't go to my Senior Prom, or my Junior Prom, for that matter. (It surprises the Brits when I tell them that The Senior Prom is taken so seriously in the States that they actually have a "junior" practice session that serves as a dress rehearsal for the real thing.) I was a dweeb—before anyone knew what a dweeb was—but such is the mystique of The Prom that I, bereft of a girlfriend, was encouraged to find an unattached girl to ask to the prom, just so we wouldn't miss out on the experience. This is (or was in my day) a common practice, and gave rise to the not untrue notion of geeks having to take their cousins to the prom.

Incidentally, I declined to do this. A bit churlish of me, I admit, but I had been the sort of dweeb bigger kids—that would be all of them; I was an exceptionally tiny child—took pleasure in jamming into lockers while they kicked my books down the hallway, so after four years of that I pretty much felt all of them could go screw themselves. And, oddly, that's what they did, which leads nicely to the next paragraph.

Prom virgin though I was, I still heard stories of riotous nights out. Most Senior Prom revelers didn't return home until the following morning, and it was an open secret that Prom Night was the traditional occasion for losing your virginity. (As a non-prom attendee, several more years came and went before I managed to misplace mine.)

I realize times have changed, and the 15 year olds going to the British Proms probably have as hard a time recalling the distant memory of their lost their virginity as their 18-year-old American counterparts do now, but the idea of an American prom being the first true adult experience in a young person's life is, in my view what separates the two, and makes what happens here little more than an expensive teenage dance.

That said, British teens will continue to hold a "Prom" but, as with their sorry attempts to make Trick-or-Treating part of the Halloween tradition, no one will be quite sure why. The certain thing is, until a geeky British teen is forced to take his cousin to the dance, they will never be able to claim it holds anywhere near the social implications of the true and original American Senior Prom.

Modern Inconvenience

Having just returned from Devon, I am struck afresh by the enthusiasm the larger towns in Britain show in allowing (no, insisting) on technology to enhance their life.

Just today, a bustling Saturday morning in our little market town, I visited the bank where I used a machine to deposit money (okay, then I needed to go see a teller because the machine wouldn't take the check, but stay with me here) then we went to the post office where machines for posting mail have been made available (they are remarkable mostly for their complexity and the frequency that they are out of order) and, if we had stopped at Sainsbury's, we could have checked ourselves out at the automatic tills.

Ignore what really happened for a moment and consider this: we had the opportunity to fulfill various necessary errands yet not interact with a single human being. That's a lot like being able to contact a growing number of businesses we are required to interact with yet not being able to talk to an actual person. And I have noticed a growing trend on Internet sites, as well, to fob you off on automated support staff represented by a photo of a pretty blonde with a dubious name like Mandi.

None of this is particularly new, but recent trips to the twee village of Totnes have reminded me that it has not always been this way, and that the other way, to my memory, was not so onerous that I craved the convenience of a soulless machine to speed me on my way.

All of this strikes me as a bit American, as they characteristically have the sort of short-sighted impatience that would cause someone to think, "I'm wasting my time standing here allowing this check-out girl to ring up my groceries; I could do it faster myself." The Brits, I should think, would welcome the few minutes of down time and the chance of a brief chat with the clerk but they are grabbing at this type of technology with an alacrity that puts the Americans to shame.

I've said this before, but allow me to reiterate: I work in technology, my business is computers, I was on the cutting edge back when it was slick with the blood of unfortunates clinging to their IBM Selectrics. These days, however, I feel like an ageing gunfighter, haunted by the ghosts of the men he's left dead. The technology I embraced has changed the world—radically and unequivocally—for the better, but more and more the down sides are beginning to show themselves (in the project management world we call them "dis-benefits," as in the dis-benefits of the proliferation of the automobile are the tens of thousands of people they kill every year and the fact that they are choking our planet to death, but you have to weigh that against the fact that I can get a Domino's pizza delivered in under 10 minutes).

One of those dis-benefits is going on your errands yet never interacting with a human being. My wife will have nothing to do with this, and I cannot fault her logic:

"Why should I go to an automatic till," she asks. "I still have to queue, it doesn't save me any time—they usually have to come over and approve a purchase for beer anyway—and all I've accomplished is putting someone out of a job."

She goes on to say that, for some older people, going to the shops and interacting with people, no matter how briefly, is all the social activity they get. Now my wife is more attuned to the disadvantages of the elderly due to her job—she manages several day centers that provide, among other things, a social outlet for elderly people—but old is what we are all going to be someday (unless we check out early) and if the proliferation of technology carries on this way, we're all in danger of becoming the type of person who is so out of touch with actual people that our passing goes unnoticed until the neighbors start to complain about the smell.

I guess the only thing for it, when I do get to that age, is to move to Devon.

More Separate Than You Think

    "Two people separated by a common language"

I can't tell you how many times that has been quoted to me. The quote generally arrives with an air of originality and a specious origin; I've heard it attributed to Winston Churchill, Oscar Wilde and even Shakespeare, though research (i.e. a quick look on Google) indicates that George Bernard Shaw is the person most people believe it originated with and, in Cyberland, that counts as fact.

Whoever said it, everyone has heard it, but unless you actually live and work as a Brit in the US or vice versa, you cannot begin to know how true it is.

Almost everyone, even if they don't know any expats or watch the British version of *The Office*, can effuse about the basics: "They call an elevator a 'lift' and a car hood a 'bonnet'; isn't that cute?"

Even the startling dissimilarity between the British and American use of the word "Fanny" has been so widely publicized that any visiting Yank who brings dinner conversation to a halt by inadvisably using it deserves the awkward silence that will surely follow. (Incidentally, "fanny" is falling out of favor in the US. I heard it a lot growing up but, in the last ten years I lived there, I don't recall anyone calling out, "Hey, get your fanny over here!" when trying to gain the attention of a friend. "Fanny" is now consigned to the name of your maiden aunt and a brand of chocolates made by Ms Farmer.)

If you move over here from there (or there from here) these egregious differences are quickly dispensed with, and then you get down to the nuts-and-bolts of daily life where, if you stopped to remark on every little difference, you would never get out of your house. Becoming truly bilingual is a long process, well beyond the scope of Expat English 101. (For you Brits, that's an Americanism meaning "Basic English." See what I mean.)

Here are just a few words that occur in everyday conversation and that, in the interest of just getting on with it, I do not stop to remark on. I merely make a mental note of the word, file it away and decide to either use it in the future so I can blend in or resist adopting it so I can remain an obnoxious American—but that's my personal issue and you don't need to worry about that, you just need to look at the words:

There are no commercials on British TV, they have adverts. My wife and I don't go to the movies, we go to the cinema. Going to the theater may mean going to see a play, or it may mean you are going in for an operation; if you are heading to surgery, then you are just going to visit your doctor, only it would be your GP.

They do not use scotch tape over here, they use Sellotape (and it's nowhere near as good). If you wash the dishes you are doing the washing up, and don't forget your marigolds, which is what they call dishwashing gloves. They have cling film instead of Saran Wrap (and they are welcome to it, along with the Sellotape) and they don't vacuum, they hoover.

Oddly, a bicycle is called a push bike to distinguish it from a bike, which is a motorcycle, while in the States we seem unconfused by using "bike" for both.

You don't put on your blinker or use your turn signal, you indicate. And if the car in front of you is going too slow and you want to get around it, you overtake. And if you are driving a station wagon, be sure to call it an estate car.

The stuff you throw out is rubbish, not garbage and you put it in a dust bin for the bin men to come and collect. If you have a lot of rubbish, you need a dumpster, which they call a skip.

Bollards are small cement or metal pillars spaced around pedestrian areas or along sidewalks to keep people from driving on them. I'd never heard that word while living in the US and I cannot think of a US equivalent. I run into a fair number of those types of words here.

Then there are words that sound the same, are used the same, but are spelled wrong: Curb/Kerb, Check/Cheque, Tire /Tyre and so on.

There are also words we use the same but pronounce differently: Basil, Oregano, Jaguar, Glacier, Geyser to name a few. (For a complete list with pronunciations, see your local travel agent; I think six weeks in Doncaster should get you started.)

Another jarring language tick the Brits have is a penchant for shortening words: If you are going to visit someone and they told you to bring your cossie, what would you think? Probably not that they were referring to your bathing suit. You might also puzzle over them wanting to show you a piccie of their child, or give you a prezzie.

I could, I am afraid, go on, and on, and on, so I'll wrap up by advising that, no matter how long you live here (or there) and how bilingual you think you've become, you can, and will, continue to be bushwhacked by the language.

Just last week I walked into my local pub and my pub mate greeted me with, "Hi! Are you here for your Ruby Murray?"

I'll leave it there, so you can remain as confused as I was.

Milestones

I just passed a milestone. (Really, it wasn't as painful as it sounds.)

Last night, while I was searching through my computer folder, looking for files I had forgotten about so I could update them and forget them again (this is one of the many methods I employ to avoid writing) I opened a spreadsheet entitled "HOMES".

This, as you might suspect, is a list of all the places I have ever lived, complete with addresses, rent or mortgage amounts, the exact number of days at each location and a complex rating system that I set up long ago—and no longer understand myself—that analyses factors such as storage space, porch size, number of rooms, location of the nearest swimming pool, et al, and combines them into an overall Quality of Life Ranking. (This particular spreadsheet is for my previous residences, but there are others, oh yes.)

I realize the fact that I maintain such a file hints at tantalizing personality issues, but these are best explored in another book. For the time being, let us leave speculation about why I keep such a file to the trained psychologists among you and, for the sake of expediency, just accept the fact that I do.

The file revealed that I have lived in this particular flat for 2,946 days—two days longer than the previous, US contender: the home I shared with a former girlfriend I now refer to as She-Who-Must-Not-Be-Named. (There's a little more fodder for you trained psychologists to chew on.)

But the point I am wavering toward, on this sunny and summery Sussex morning, is how smoothly, enjoyably and even serenely these years have passed. In walking to the bus stop, I marveled (as indeed I do nearly every morning) at how fetching this town is, and how it is just about as different as it could be from the soulless suburb I left behind. While I certainly enjoyed a magnanimous yard in America, and benefited from a wooded back lot and a safe, quiet neighborhood to wander around in, the place had no character—not an ounce. Nor did the town it was attached to, which was basically a collection of similar developments loosely linked together by a school district, ZIP code and a sad little shopping mall that served as a sort of town center, all of it built within the past twenty years.

Compare that to a medieval market town, listed in the Doomsday Book, with architecture dating back to the 1300s and a rich history dating back even further. Now I suppose if I was trapped in the seventh circle of relationship hell, as I was in my previous life, I might not feel as kindly toward this town, but I still could not deny its charm.

And, to be fair, the suburb did have allure, and could hold you in thrall the way a stunningly beautiful but vacuous model might: for a while, it would feel like a dream just to be in her company, but soon the thin shell of aesthetic pleasantness would be unable to overcome the fact that there was nothing else on offer. So, yes, it was green and pleasant, but the greenery had the look of a golf course; there were no hedgerows, no untamed rhododendron bushes, no wildflowers in the verges and certainly no one turning their lawn into an intricate garden billowing with blossoms and surrounded by shrubs. That would have looked too shocking amid the tidy, trim lawns and the rouge gardener would likely have been ordered to return the plot to its former, flat self.

And although there was a pool and play area nearby for use of the residents, when I brought my autistic son there, he was regarded as too, well, not like the others, and maybe he would be happier playing elsewhere.

So, yeah, beauty and convenience are no guarantee of a high quality of life.

Strange then that I gave that place a ranking of 22 and my current home an 18. I must have rated it when I was thinking like an American and still believed happiness was measured in direct proportion to the amount of available storage space and that joy increased with the size of your porch. Realizing that contentment does not come from external factors is an important lesson, one I spent long and painful years learning. So rediscovering my futile attempt to quantify happiness was fortuitous and timely, and served as yet another reminder that—despite understandable concerns at the time—I made the right decision after all.

It's been many years since I have been unhappy, and some time since I have thought about how comparatively happy or unhappy I have been during the various periods of my life, regardless of swimming pools, spare rooms, closet size or expansive patios. I am happy here, and content with my postage stamp sized balcony, modest flat and the woman I traveled thousands of miles—far from everything and everyone I knew—to marry.

Britain has been good to me, it's a wondrous place, full of history, pleasant scenery and good beer, and if I occasionally feel a twinge of nostalgia for the life I left behind, I always come back to this final, defining truth: I am not living thousands of miles away from home, I am home.

Glossary

Anorak: Literally, a parka-type coat with a hood. Due to their popularity among Trainspotters, the term has come to mean a geek or nerd or anyone with an obsessive interest in a narrow field.

ASBO: (Pronounced AS' bo.) Acronym for Anti-Social Behavior Order, a law designed to assist those who, previously, could aspire to be no more than obnoxious by enabling them to become full-fledged criminals. It is regarded as insulting to real criminals, who spent years learning their craft only to find their fraternity infiltrated by fifteen-year olds who played their iPods too loudly.

Backslang: Speak words backwards. Like *Rhyming Slang*, it was originally used as a means of secret communication between street gangs.

Bank Holiday: A holiday involving a day off from work.

Berk: Cockney rhyming slang meaning "idiot." Shortened form of Berkley Hunt; you figure it out.

Bird: A female. Generally young and pretty.

BNP: The British National Party. Neo-Nazis masquerading as a political party.

Bodge: To fix something shoddily or in an unprofessional manner.

Bog: Public toilet, and not a nice one.

Bog Standard: Basic.

Car Park: A parking lot, and not, as I first imagined, a place where cars went to play.

Chips: Fries.

Cinema: The movies

Chav: Aggressive teenagers, of working class background, who engage in anti-social behavior such as street drinking, drug abuse and rowdiness. Back in the day, we called them *Yobs*.

Crisps: Potato Chips.

DIY: Do-It-Yourself, the national mania surrounding fixing your house up. Usually results in a *bodge*.

Dodgy: Shady, suspect or shoddy, as in a dodgy deal, a dodgy car or a dodgy knee (as in trick knee).

Double Glazed: Double paned windows.

Estate Car: A station wagon.

Flat: Apartment.

Fortnight: Two weeks.

Glasgow Kiss: A head butt.

Holiday: Vacation.

Hoover: To vacuum.

Jumper: A sweater.

Knickers: Women's underwear. In the US, short pants are sometimes referred to as "Knickers" which is the diminutive of "Knickerbockers." It is not a good thing, in England, to say to a male companion who happens to be clad in shorts, "Oh, I see you're wearing your knickers."

Knickerbocker Glory: Basically, an Ice Cream Sundae.

Loo: Toilet. Also: *bog*.

NHS: The National Health Service.

Penultimate: Second to the last. Brits like this word for some reason, probably for the same reason they like to say words like *fortnight*.

Piccie: Photograph.

Pitch: Playing field.

Queue: A line. Brits don't "stand in line," they "queue up."

Quid: A pound. The monetary unit, not the weight measure.

Rollie: Hand-rolled cigarette.

Sod's Law: Often described as the British equivalent of Murphy's Law, it is actually, subtly different. Murphy's Law is a bona fide design theory that states, "If there is more than one possible outcome for a job or task, and one of those outcomes will result in disaster or an undesirable consequence, then somebody will do it that way." Sod's Law leans more toward the inevitability of rain if you wash your car or organize a picnic.

Spinnaker Tower: Originally called the Millennium Tower, the project began in 1995 to be finished by year 2000. Construction did not begin, however, until 2001, which is why it was renamed the Spinnaker Tower. The project was eventually completed 6 years behind schedule and massively over budget.

Stone: British unit of weight equaling 14 pounds.

Take the Piss: To make good natured fun of. Also called "Taking the Michael" or "Taking the Mickey" out of someone.

Till: The checkout counter in a store.

Trainspotting: Literally, spotting trains. Honest, people stand around all day on railway platforms in their anoraks, with sandwiches and flasks of tea, writing down the registration numbers of every train that goes by. Sometimes they take photos and record the sound of the engines. Don't try to understand it; it's a uniquely British phenomenon.

Yob: A young delinquent. Yob is *backslang* for Boy.

About the Author

Michael Harling grew up in rural Columbia County in Upstate New York. He moved to the UK in March 2002 and has been recording his observations of the indigenous population on his popular blog *Postcards From Across the Pond* ever since.

Michael is the father of three sons from a previous marriage. He currently lives in Horsham with his wife, Shonagh

More Postcards From Across the Pond is his second book.

For Michael's blog, website and contact details, visit:
www.michaelharling.com

http://michaelharling.com
Sussex, United Kingdom

Made in the USA
Columbia, SC
16 January 2018